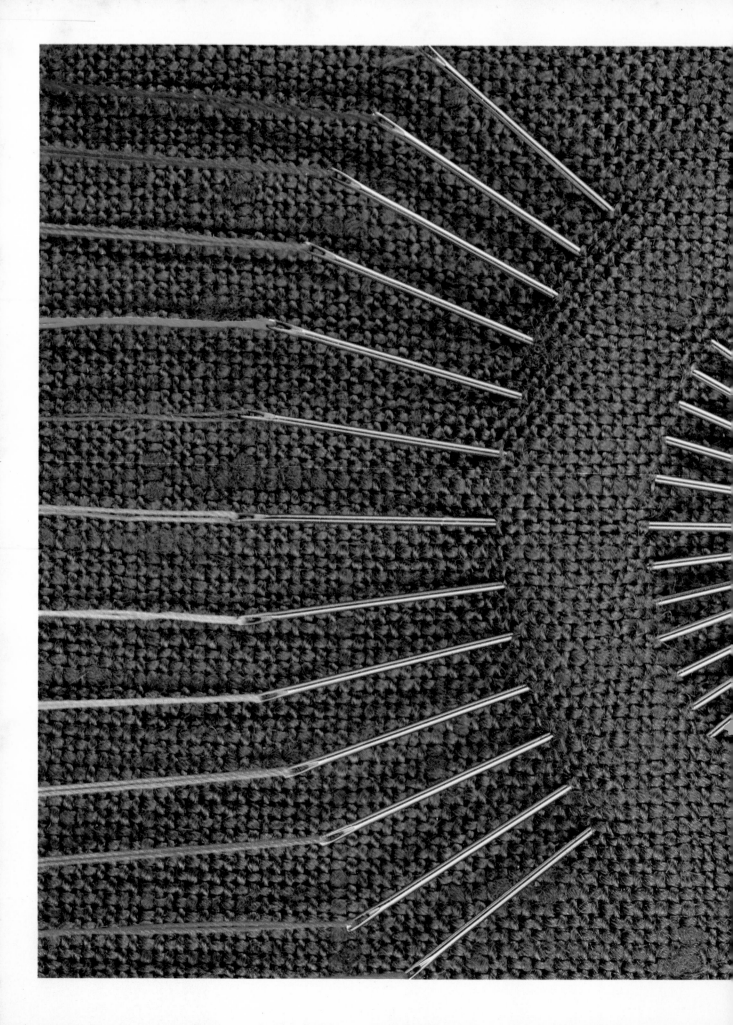

Family Circle

MAKING YOUR OWN CLOTHES

Albany Books

Designed and produced by
Albany Books
36 Park Street London W1Y 4DE

First published 1979

Published by Albany Books

Copyright © Albany Books 1979

Printed in Hong Kong

ISBN 0 86136 085 0

*This text has previously been
published in issues of* Family Circle.
*The publishers wish to thank the
Editor and staff of the magazine for
their help in preparing it for this
edition. They also gratefully
acknowledge the loan of
transparencies from* Family Circle.

*Design : Walker Pinfold Associates
Picture Research : Raj Sacranie*

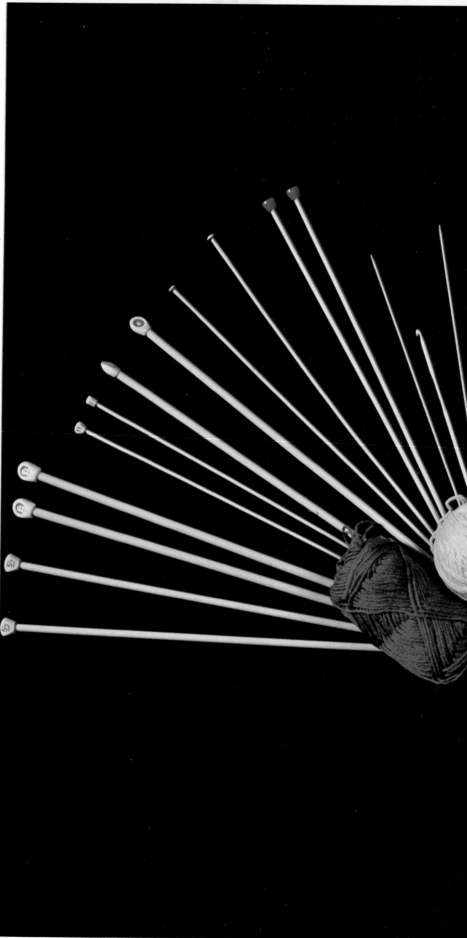

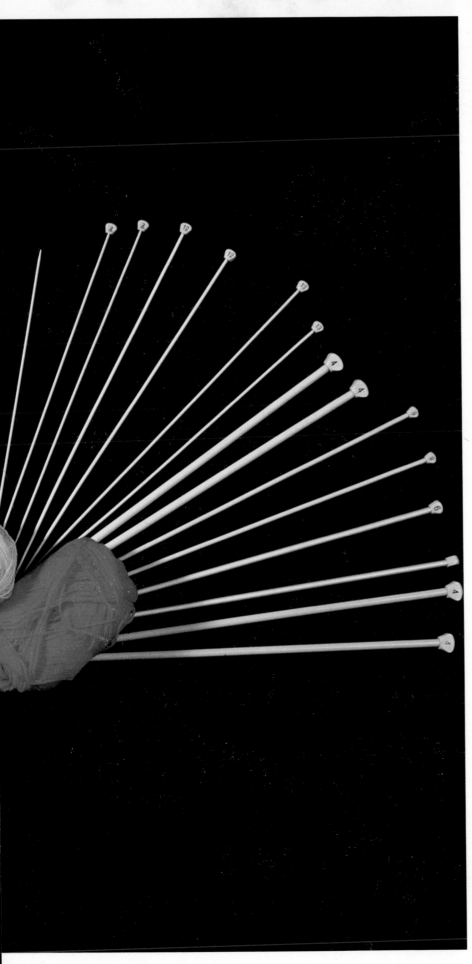

Contents

Dressmaking

Step by step to good dressmaking

Choosing your pattern and fabric

Making clothes at home can be a relaxing pastime, and can save money. But if you aren't sure what style you should choose and, having bought your pattern, can't think what fabric to use, then costly mistakes can be made. Keep the following basic fashion rules in mind when you next choose a pattern and fabric.

If you are short and plump, choose patterns that are easy fitting, have long, unbroken lines from shoulder to hem, and keep to one-colour outfits, to make you look taller. *Avoid* pleats and gathers around waist and hipline, wide or contrasting belts, separates and anything too tight-fitting.

If you are pear-shaped (small bust, wide hips), choose styles with some fullness in the bodice. Jackets should be hip-length and not too waisted, separates should have lighter or brighter tops, with darker skirts that are smooth but not too tight over the hips. *Avoid* tightly-belted styles, hip pockets, wide cuffs, tight or bunchy skirts.

If you are top heavy (large bust, narrow hips), go for well-cut tops, with curved, vertical seaming over the bust, slim sleeves; skirts should flare slightly, jackets and coats should be single-breasted and slightly flared. Wear overblouses or tunics, rather than tucked-in tops. *Avoid* tightly-fitted tops, frills, pleats, gathers above or below the bust.

If you are too tall and too thin, choose softly-bloused tops, polo necks, scarf collars, full sleeves. Jackets can be three-quarter length, belted and pocketed. Skirts can be flared, gathered or A-line. *Avoid* waist-length jackets, tight clinging dresses, vertical stripes, frilly styles.

If you are short and petite, choose narrow shapes, small collars or plain, round necklines. Jackets should be fairly short, skirts slightly flared or finely pleated. Choose same-colour separates to add height. Wear sweaters and blouses tucked in, slim trousers. *Avoid* chunky jackets and skirts, wide sleeves.

If you are tall and big, pick tailored styles, not too fitted, wide collars, scooped-out necklines, smoothly set-in sleeves, straightish skirts. In separates, choose very long shirts or tunics rather than bulky sweaters, and straight-legged trousers. *Avoid* full sleeves, jutting pockets and heavy cuffs.

Having decided on your pattern style, you should now think about a suitable fabric. Most paper pattern companies print a list of suggested fabrics on the back of each pattern envelope; these give an idea of the *type* of fabric suited to the design. Take your pattern with you when you choose your fabric, and don't skimp on the amount you buy: this is important with checks and large prints, where seams have to be matched. As a guide, here are some points that might help you if you are uncertain about fabric choice. A style with interesting seaming will look best in plain-coloured, firm fabric. A plain, very simple style can take a print or plaid. A design with gathers, draping or smocking must have a fabric that falls in soft, graceful folds. A pattern with pressed pleats must have a fabric solid and firm enough to press well: fabrics containing a high percentage of synthetic fibre will press into pleats that stay crisp after laundering. Full, gathered sleeves aren't successful with a fabric that is too soft: they'll flop and won't show their true shape. Choose a slightly crisp-feeling fabric, either silk, synthetic, or fine cotton, which will hold its shape when bunched up in your hand, yet will be fine enough to gather effectively.

If you are a beginner, choose an easy-to-handle fabric, such as a firm cotton, either plain or with a small print, or a medium-weight, firm wool. Don't choose anything too cheap: better fabrics usually handle more easily. Avoid slippery, silky fabrics, soft jerseys, velvet, one-way prints, stretch fabrics and chiffons.

Measuring up

It's important to realize, when buying a pattern, that the sizes given in the tables of measurements on patterns and in the catalogues are *body measurements,* not the actual size of the pattern: the pattern tissues are always cut larger, to allow for ease of movement. As a general guide to size selection for dresses, blouses and coats, buy the nearest pattern size to your *bust* measurement: it's usually easier to adjust the waist and hip size than the upper part. For skirts and trousers, buy a pattern nearest to your *hip* measurement and adjust the waist, if necessary, by taking in or letting out seams and darts. Whenever possible, choose multi-size patterns which include a choice of size lines printed on each pattern sheet.

First of all, take all your measurements accurately. Make yourself a measurement chart, with columns for your own and the pattern measurements, plus space for adjustment notes. Measure at the following points: **Bust:** around fullest part. **Waist:** with tape held in firmly. **High hipline:** around hip bones, about 7·5cm from waistline. **Hips:** around fullest part of seat. **Shoulder:** from side of neck to tip of shoulder. **Outside arm length:** from tip of shoulder to elbow, then on to wrist. **Underarm to waist. Around top arm:** largest part. **Around forearm:** midway between elbow and wrist. **Around wrist. Across back:** armhole to armhole. **Back waist length:** from centre back base of neck to waist. **Skirt length:** from centre back of waist to hem. **Front shoulder to waist:** measure over the bust. **Front neck to waist:** from base of neck. **Front waist to hem.**

Having bought the pattern size nearest to your main measurements, select all the pieces you need to make up the chosen version. Unless your measurements have conformed exactly to the table of sizes given on your pattern, this is the moment to make any slight adjustment to the tissues, *before* cutting out, to save you from the frustration of trying to make your garment fit after you have laboriously made it up.

Measure the main pattern sections (bodice, skirt, sleeves) at all the points you have noted on your

Arrange pattern pieces on fabric

own chart. Measure only from stitching line to stitching line, omitting seams and darts. Jot down the pattern measurements in pencil, beside your own measurements, to determine whether any changes need to be made. Remember though, that bust and hip sections should be *at least* 5cm larger, and a fitted waist 1cm larger than your own measurements, to allow you to move around in the finished garment. (This is described on patterns, as 'ease'.)

If there does appear to be a great difference between the pattern's measurements and yours, pin up the darts and seams of your pattern pieces as they are to be assembled, then try on, slipping your arm carefully through the armhole. (Do not try to fit the sleeve pattern, as it could tear.)

Having tried on your half-pattern, check on these points:
1. Centre lines of front and back: they should be hanging absolutely straight; pin the paper to your slip or dress, to hold it in place.
2. Shoulder seam length.
3. Neckline shape.
4. Dart positions: they must point towards the fullest part of the figure. At this stage, mark any new direction lines with pins.
5. Bodice length and width (or waist position, if the pattern is an all-in-one style).

Make notes of any adjustments needed. After removing pattern, mark darts again, where necessary, using coloured pencil and ruler. If pattern is too long, make tucks across the tissue; if too short, insert extra paper strips. (On printed paper patterns, you will find that lengthening and shortening lines are marked for your guidance.) A few further pattern adjustments are shown in diagrams A to G.

Getting ready to cut
Now you are almost ready to take the big step and put scissors to fabric. There are one or two more things to do first, though.
Straightening the grain: To ensure that a garment will hang properly, attention must be paid to the fabric grain. Before cutting, make sure the ends are straight, at right angles to selvedges. To straighten, snip into the selvedge near the end of the fabric and try tearing it across the width, or pull out a thread across the width (near the end) and cut across, following the drawn line. If the ends still don't lie square naturally, although they seem to be straight across the grain, pull the fabric diagonally, from the shortest corners, to straighten.
Shrinking: Most well-known makes of fabric are pre-shrunk during manufacture, but if you cannot check on this when you buy the fabric, it is advisable to test before making up. To do this, snip the selvedges at intervals along the length of cloth. Fold it in half lengthwise, right sides inside, and pin selvedges together. Note the doubled width, from fold to selvedges. Then damp-press a 15cm-deep section right across the width, and leave on the board to cool and dry out thoroughly. Re-measure. If any shrinkage has occurred, and the fabric is *not washable,* damp-press the entire length and allow it to dry out completely on a flat surface before cutting out.

To pre-shrink *washable* fabrics, straighten ends first and tack the

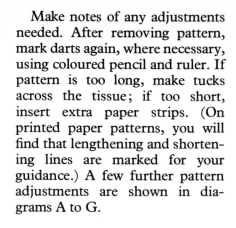

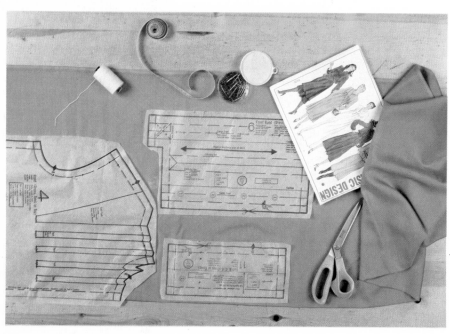

doubled length of fabric across the ends and down the selvedges. Immerse, in flat folds, into a large bowl full of cool-to-lukewarm plain water and leave for several hours. Spin out excess water, or squeeze out carefully by hand (do not wring), then drip dry, smoothing out the fabric as flat and square as possible, so that it will dry smoothly. Press, if necessary, before cutting out. *Synthetic* fibre fabrics will not shrink, and you should not attempt to pre-shrink crêpes.

Layouts: These are the 'plans' printed on the pattern instruction sheet, and they are your guide to the way the pattern pieces should be placed. On certain fabrics, it is necessary to place pattern pieces all facing the same direction: 'one-way' fabrics include those that have a print with motifs facing in

one direction only, and napped or pile fabrics, such as velvet and fur fabric. When you place all pattern pieces in one direction, it is known as cutting out 'with nap'. If a pattern does not include a 'with nap' layout and fabric requirement, it may be necessary to allow extra fabric, to enable you to place the pattern pieces facing the same way. (It is advisable for beginners to avoid one-way fabrics.)

When cutting out, work on a large flat surface. Smooth out the fabric (press, if necessary); make sure that it is wrong side up and, if working with a double layer, pin the selvedges together down the entire length. Mark the layout that applies to your size group, fabric width and the version you are making; follow this carefully when positioning the tissues.

Press creases out of the pattern

tissues and trim away any excess margins of tissue. Arrange pattern pieces as shown on your chosen layout. The lengthwise grain lines marked on your pattern with a ruled line, or with a line of large holes, *must* be placed parallel to the selvedges, to ensure that your garment will hang correctly: use a ruler to check this and pin the pattern at each end of the straight grain line to secure. Pin the rest of the piece in place along stitching lines. Check that every piece you need is pinned on.

Now you are ready to cut. Using sharp shears, cut with long, even strokes, placing one hand flat on pattern and fabric, to keep them steady. When you come to the notches around the pattern edges, cut them outwards if there is

Examples of pattern adjustments

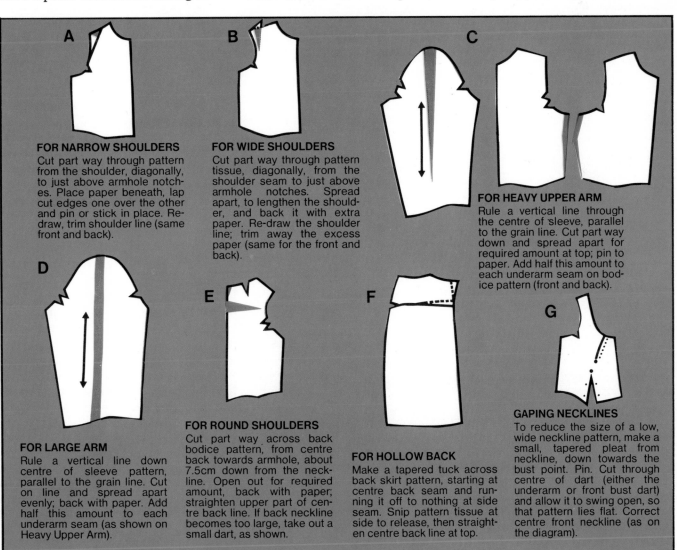

A

FOR NARROW SHOULDERS
Cut part way through pattern from the shoulder, diagonally, to just above armhole notches. Place paper beneath, lap cut edges one over the other and pin or stick in place. Re-draw, trim shoulder line (same front and back).

B

FOR WIDE SHOULDERS
Cut part way through pattern tissue, diagonally, from the shoulder seam to just above armhole notches. Spread apart, to lengthen the shoulder, and back it with extra paper. Re-draw the shoulder line; trim away the excess paper (same for the front and back).

C

FOR HEAVY UPPER ARM
Rule a vertical line through the centre of sleeve, parallel to the grain line. Cut part way down and spread apart for required amount at top; pin to paper. Add half this amount to each underarm seam on bodice pattern (front and back).

D

FOR LARGE ARM
Rule a vertical line down centre of sleeve pattern, parallel to the grain line. Cut on line and spread apart evenly; back with paper. Add half this amount to each underarm seam (as shown on Heavy Upper Arm).

E

FOR ROUND SHOULDERS
Cut part way across back bodice pattern, from centre back towards armhole, about 7.5cm down from the neckline. Open out for required amount, back with paper; straighten upper part of centre back line. If back neckline becomes too large, take out a small dart, as shown.

F

FOR HOLLOW BACK
Make a tapered tuck across back skirt pattern, starting at centre back seam and running it off to nothing at side seam. Snip pattern tissue at side to release, then straighten centre back line at top.

G

GAPING NECKLINES
To reduce the size of a low, wide neckline pattern, make a small, tapered pleat from neckline, down towards the bust point. Pin. Cut through centre of dart (either the underarm or front bust dart) and allow it to swing open, so that pattern lies flat. Correct centre front neckline (as on the diagram).

enough space or mark with coloured thread before removing your pattern pieces.

Next, transfer all the markings from the pattern through to both layers of fabric. The two best methods are tailor-tacking (suitable for all fabrics) and pins and chalk (for smooth-surfaced fabrics only). Whichever method you use, always run a single tacking line along all folds, to mark the centre of the section when opened out.

Tailor-tacking: Thread a long length of cotton (double, but don't knot ends). Take two stitches, at the same point, through the pattern marking and both layers of fabric at the same time, leaving a 1cm loop and two 2·5cm ends of cotton (diagram H). Continue in this way at all marked points on stitching lines. When all the necessary tacks have been made, snip through the centre of each loop. Take off the pattern tissue, then separate the two fabric layers, carefully snipping the connecting threads as you go, to give identical markings on each garment section.

Pins and chalk: Pin through all pattern markings and both layers of fabric. Turn work over to reverse side and run the sharp edge of a piece of tailor's chalk between the pins. Turn work back to the pattern side, fold back edge of tissue and chalk the fabric on this side at pinned positions.

Fitting: Even if you have made up a certain pattern previously, it is still advisable to tack the main pieces together and try on before doing any stitching, particularly if using a different type of fabric. Don't be tempted to start stitching any special design details, such as yokes and pockets, before fitting, but do check that their *positions* are correct.

Tacking, as a preparation for fitting, is important, as you cannot fit satisfactorily or accurately by pinning. For the best results, tack all darts and seams, using smallish stitches, starting and finishing securely, so that seams will not come apart when you try on the garment. For the first fitting, tack only the main parts of the garment together. Tack the sleeve seams, but do not set the sleeves into the armholes.

Start with darts. Working on the wrong side of the fabric, pin and tack all darts carefully, from base to point. Then, with right sides together, pin and tack all main seams, taking care to match all markings, so that exact seam allowances are maintained. When tacking a curved edge to a straight one, ease the excess fabric on the curved edge evenly, placing pins at right angles to the seam line, before you tack. Leave any openings for fastenings untacked, but if there is to be a long centre-back zip, tack it in place: it will make fitting much easier, particularly if you have no helper.

Try on the tacked garment, right way out, in front of a full-length mirror. Pin any openings together, matching centre lines and lapping them one over the other, as they will be worn. Look for the following points.

Centre front and back lines or seams should hang at right angles to the floor, as should side seams.

Darts should all point to fullest parts of figure and take up the right amount of fabric, so that they do not drag or set up folds elsewhere.

Waistline or any waist shaping must come in the right place.

Buttonholes, pocket positions and other design details: check that these will come in the right places for your proportions; mark any new positions with pins.

General fit and comfort of garment: If any section seems too large, pin out an equal amount on each side. Do not fit too closely, however; you must be able to move around in your finished garment. Sit down in skirts or trousers to make sure that you can do this without undue strain on the fabric. *Make a note* of any parts that are too tight or mark the area with pins, rather than trying to re-pin while the garment is on.

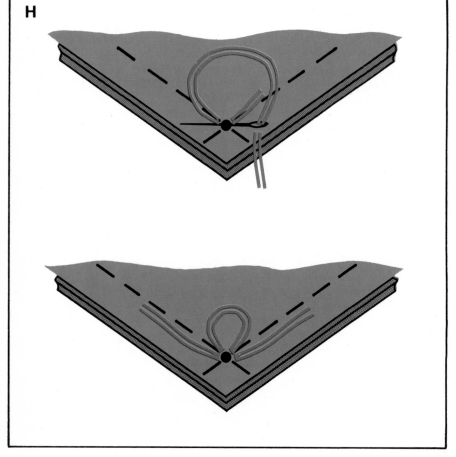

Getting ready to cut

Sleeves: Slip the correct tacked sleeve on to one arm. Pin to bodice at shoulder and underarm only, at this stage, and check size by bending the elbow. See that any fullness or darts come in the right position for the elbow.

Correcting faults: If the centre lines swing in one direction, lift and pin a deeper seam on the *opposite* side, either at waistline or shoulder. If darts do not point towards the fullest part, mark the new direction with a line of pins. If the darts need deepening, pin to give a smooth effect. If waistline position is wrong, mark the new line. If side seams swing towards the front, lift and pin the back waist seam; if they swing towards the back, lift and deepen the front waist seam.

Remove the garment, then note any adjustments. On the inside, use tailor's chalk to mark any new stitching lines, chalking along the backs of the pins. Remove pins, then mark these lines with thread. Now start making up your garment following the pattern instructions, stitching and pressing as you go. Stitch, press and finish fitted sleeves (with the exception of the lower edges) and tack them into the armholes. If a collar is being used, turn under and tack outer edges of one layer, then tack the neck edge to the garment neckline, matching centres.

Try on the garment again, pinning together any openings as before, and check all fitting points once more. Turn under the lower edges of sleeves and pin at desired length. Check that the collar looks right and that the width will be correct when finished. When the garment has been fitted to your satisfaction, you can go ahead and complete each stage of making up.

Choosing the right interfacing:

This is a layer of special material (often called interlining), which is placed between the outer fabric and its facing, and usually cut from the facing pattern. Its purpose is to hold, permanently, the shape of a section, to reinforce areas that may get a lot of wear or to add crispness to collars and cuffs.

The type of interfacing to use depends on the weight, texture and character of your fabric and whether you want the section stiffened or softly shaped. Before buying, try pieces of the various types between two layers of your fabric to test the effect. Ideally, your interfacing material should be no thicker than the outside fabric. If your garment is to be washable, you must choose a washable interfacing, too.

Woven interfacings range from lightweight linen and stiffened cotton to heavier canvases for use in tailored garments. (Some of these are washable.) Non-woven interfacings come in a number of different weights and thicknesses, some specially made for use with synthetics. They can be washed or dry-cleaned and, as they have no grain, can be cut in any direction.

Iron-on interfacings are also available in various weights and types to suit all fabrics. Use the heavier weight iron-on interfacings for small areas only.

Sewing Machines

A good machine will give years of excellent service if well treated and looked after. Care of your machine is most important whether it's old or brand new. You can keep it in trim yourself between professional overhauls, and the instruction book will show exactly where to apply the oil. Do buy special sewing machine oil: this is very fine and is the only type suited to the delicate mechanism. Before oiling, all dust and lint must be removed, otherwise it will clog and your machine's running will be hampered. Keep the bobbin dust-free by using a special soft brush. After each sewing session take out the bobbin and brush all around the case and moving parts underneath. After dusting, then oiling at the points shown in your instruction book, run the machine fast to allow the oil to circulate, then clean it down thoroughly with a piece of lint-free cloth; leave a folded tissue or several layers of clean cloth under the lowered pressure foot to absorb any excess oil. Keep the machine covered when not in use; if it is stored in a cold room, move it into a warm atmosphere for a while before using, to allow the oil to become free-moving; do not store the machine too near a source of heat, such as a radiator.

If you are thinking of buying a new machine, it is important to know what types are available and to find out just what they will do. Today's new machines fall into three main categories: the *straight stitch*, the *plain zigzag*, and the semi and fully *automatics*. The type for you depends on what your sewing needs are likely to be. For instance, if you just want a machine for plain sewing in the home, for mending and making the occasional garment, then a *straight stitch* machine may fill your requirements. These stitch only in a straight line, usually forward and reverse, and you may be able to find a reconditioned machine of this type at a reasonable cost.

If you intend to make clothes for yourself and family, it is well worth considering a *zigzag* or *swing needle* model. Apart from straight stitching these machines will also sew a useful zigzag stitch for speedy seam neatening and to form a close satin stitch for buttonholes and monograms. These models vary in what they can do. They usually have the facility for making some embroidery patterns and can be used for darning, and sewing on buttons.

The *automatic* machine is sophisticated, but is now so simplified that no-one should be wary of being able to operate one. Again, there are some which have more refinements than others, but most will produce countless embroidery patterns at the touch of a dial, and have built-in stretch stitches for sewing jersey and elasticated fabrics. They are, of course, the most expensive, but they almost think for themselves!

You must also decide whether to choose a 'flat-bed' or a 'free-arm' model. A free-arm machine narrows down at the needle end to a slim shape to facilitate easy sewing around cuffs and sleeves. There is usually a separate extension table which may be fitted on to make up the sewing area to full width. The flat-bed machine is made with a solid, rectangular base, giving a permanent large sewing area. These are usually heavier and may be a little cheaper.

Shop around when buying a new machine and try out any you are interested in. Check that the machine is easy to thread, that the light is in a good position over the needle, and does not glare. Try out the spool-winding device; test how slowly the machine can stitch, and how long it takes to come to a stop. Check whether straight stitching stays straight when your hands are taken off the fabric. If it is a portable model, make sure you can carry it easily when in its case. Finally, find out what kind of guarantee the machine carries; check that it is electrically safe and whether spare parts and servicing will be easily available.

Machine stitching

Accurate stitching is one of the essential requirements in dressmaking. Get to know how to use your machine properly and to its fullest advantage before you start dressmaking. If you have never used a sewing machine before, you will, of course, need a fair amount of practice before you can sew lovely straight seams. It may help to start stitching straight lines on to paper, with no thread in the machine. Place a sheet of ruled paper under the presser foot, keeping the greater part of it to the left of the needle. Stitch along the lines as accurately as you can; stitch slowly at first, increasing speed gradually. You will see by the needle holes how often you go off the straight.

When straight lines become easy to stitch, try drawing circles and curved shapes on to paper and machining around them accurately, turning the paper as you stitch. Next, try out your stitching on scraps of fabric, experimenting with different threads, to get the best effect.

Threading up: The threading sequence is very important: do it slightly in the wrong order and your machine won't sew! Follow carefully the diagram provided with your machine: you'll soon be able to do it automatically. The bobbin should be wound, by machine, before threading up the top part. Make sure you wind smoothly and don't overfill it. Also make sure that the upper thread passes *between* the tension discs (on left-hand side of front of machine immediately above needle) and that the needle itself is threaded in the right direction.

Stitching: Raise the presser foot, then turn balance wheel towards you until needle is at highest point. Take both threads under presser foot towards the back of the machine. Place fabric under presser foot, with most of it to left of needle. Turn balance wheel to lower needle into fabric, lower presser foot and position hands to guide fabric.

Start to stitch slowly, allowing the fabric to feed through naturally, to avoid stretching or puckering. When you come to a corner, stop, leaving the needle well down, and raise presser foot. Pivot fabric to new stitching direction, lower foot and resume stitching.

To remove fabric after stitching, raise needle to highest point, lift foot and pull the fabric gently back from the needle. Cut threads about 5cm from fabric and knot ends firmly before cutting off (or just go back a few stitches at beginning and end of seams, to secure, then cut threads close to fabric).

Before beginning a garment, it is advisable to test-stitch a scrap of the fabric you will be using. This will allow you to check the length of the stitch, the tension and the needle size.

Making a seam

Seams are the all-important construction lines of a garment, so they must be accurately stitched, well pressed and neat on the inside. To make a plain seam, place the two pieces to be joined, right sides together, raw edges meeting. Match notches accurately and pin fabric layers together at these points. Then pin at beginning and end of seam and between these points (see diagram I). The pins may be placed across the seam, at right angles to the stitching line, or with points towards the top of the seam, so that they can be removed easily when stitching. Slippery or difficult fabrics should be tacked before stitching. When joining two pieces of fabric which are not exactly on the straight grain, the *direction* in which you stitch is important. Always stitch from the widest to the narrowest part, to avoid distorting the grain: from hem to waist, underarm to waist, neck to shoulder. Avoid stitching on top of pins or tackings; remove pins as you go. After stitching, remove tacking thread gently.

Press along machine-stitching, with seam edges together; this helps to embed the stitches into the fabric. Then separate the layers and press the seam open, first lightly with the point of the iron, and then in the way required for the fabric. Finally, run the point of the iron along, just under the edges, to remove any imprint made through to the right side.

Raw edges must now be finished off, to prevent fraying. This can be done in several ways: overcasting, zigzagging, edge-stitching, pinking or binding; choose the one most suitable for your fabric.

Coping with sleeves

All sleeves have a back and a front, the curve of the sleeve head being shaped to fit the corresponding curves of the front and back armholes. Also, on a long fitted sleeve, the back part of the underarm seam is always longer than the front, to

Thread, Needle and Stitch Chart

| Fabric Type | Thread | Needle Sizes | | Stitches per 2·5cm |
		hand sewing	machine	
Sheer: Chiffon; fine lace; organdie, voile	Pure silk; polyester (for synthetics)	10	finest	15–20
Stretch Fabrics	Polyester; pure silk	9	fine	12–15 (use slight zig-zag stitch, if possible)
Fine: Lawn; crepe; pure silks; satin; sheer wools; thin jersey; fine cottons; lace	Pure silk; mercerised No 50; polyester (for synthetics)	9	fine	12–15
Medium: Linens; wools; rayons; silks; satin; velvet; suitings cottons; PVC	Pure silk; mercerised No 40 or 50	8	medium-fine	12
Medium Heavy: Coatings; tweeds; corduroy; felt; furnishing fabrics	Mercerised No 40	7/8	medium	10–12
Heavy: Canvas; sailcloth; furnishing fabrics	Mercerised	6/7	coarse	8–10
Leather	Pure silk	—	medium-fine	10

Sequence for pinning a seam

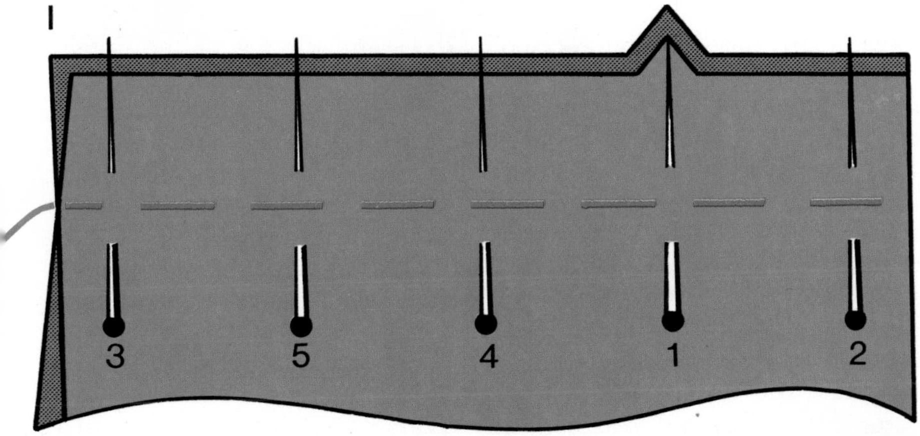

allow room for the elbow; the excess length is eased in or darted (see diagram J). So you must be sure to cut a *pair* of sleeves: if your layout suggests cutting from a single layer of fabric, you must turn the pattern over after cutting one sleeve.

Making the sleeves: Stitch small darts or gather the fullness be-tween notches at the correct elbow position, so that the back of the sleeve seam fits the front. Press darts. Complete the underarm seam; press open and neaten edges. (Do not finish the lower edge of the sleeve at this stage.)

Setting sleeves into armholes: Check that each sleeve head and armhole has the front and back notches and top point of sleeve clearly marked. Using the largest stitch on the machine, run two lines of stitching around the sleeve head, between the notches, the first on the seam line, the second 5mm above it (diagram K). Pull up carefully until the sleeve head be-comes rounded, but not actually gathered below the stitching line, then secure thread (diagram L).

Turn the bodice to the wrong side and, with the sleeve right side out, place it inside its correct armhole. Working on the sleeve side and inserting pins *across* the seam line, pin together, matching the centre of the sleeve head to the shoulder seam, underarm seams and side notches, in that order. Pin, distributing fullness evenly (diagram M), then pin the re-mainder of the sleeve in position. Tack, using small stitches, and try on before machining. Working on the sleeve side, starting at the underarm seams, stitch as far as the first notch position, then, as you come to the fuller part of the sleeve, stitch only 2·5cm or so at a time, straightening out the seam allowance before continuing, until you reach the other notch. Finish the stitching off strongly at the underarm; remove tacks and gath-ering threads. Snip the lower curve of the armhole seam, to relieve tension, if necessary. Trim seam allowances to 5mm and neaten edges.

Pressing: Pull the sleeve inside out, insert a pressing pad or sleeve board end into the armhole, then with seam edges towards the sleeve, cover work with a cloth; press carefully, pulling the sleeve out as you press, to make a clean armhole line.

Putting in a Zip

By far the easiest and smoothest way of fastening a garment is with a zip. There is a wide range avail-able: be sure to select the right weight and type for your fabric. Before inserting the zip, make sure that the opening is going to be long enough for you to be able to get in

15

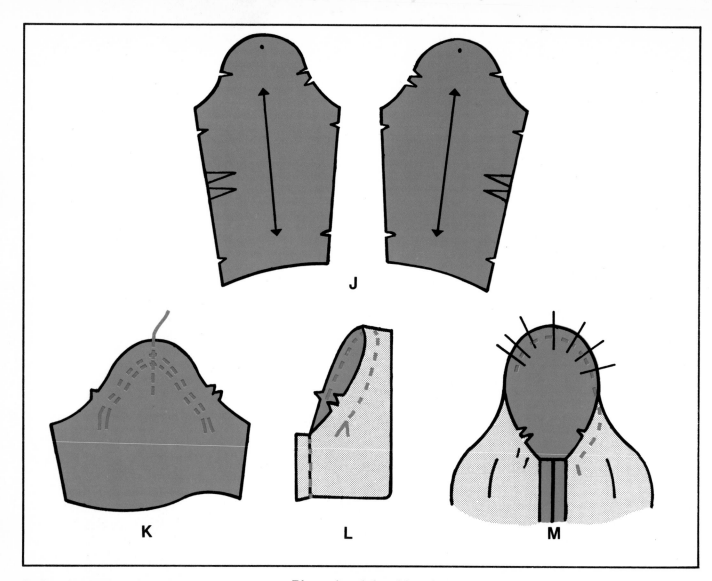

J

K   L   M

and out of the garment easily. Always leave room for a hook and eye at the top of the zip: this takes the strain and prevents it from un-zipping in wear. Keep the zip closed while you are stitching it in and while pressing, and never cut away the excess tapes at the top and bottom of the zip. If you are using a machine, replace the ordinary sewing foot with a special zipper or cording foot, to enable you to stitch close to the zip teeth. To ensure a straight line of stitching, tack in the zip accurately, then machine just to one side of the tacking.

Centre back opening: The opening should be the length of the zip, plus 2·5cm. Stitch the seam below the opening. Tack the remainder of the seam (diagram N) and press

open. Place the right side of the closed zip to the wrong side of the garment, with the centre of the zip teeth directly under the seam line and with the top of the slider 2.5cm down from the edge of the garment. Pin the zip in place from the right side, on each side of the seam line. Tack, then stitch as near as possible to the tacked seam line, starting and finishing at the top. The end can be squared or pointed (diagram O). Press and remove tacks. To finish, sew a hook and eye to the wrong side, above the zip.

Skirt opening: The opening for the zip should be the zip length plus 1.5cm. Stitch the skirt seam below the opening. Tack the re-mainder of the seam and press open. Place the right side of the closed zip to the wrong side of the tacked seam. Pin the zip behind

the seam, the top of the fastener 1.5cm below the top edge of the skirt and with the teeth to the left side of the seam line. Stitch as near as possible to the teeth on the back edge of the skirt opening, 6mm away on the front edge (diagram P). Stitch straight across the base. Press and remove tacking stitches.

Inserting the zip by hand: Follow instructions above as far as tacking the zip in place. After tacking, stitch by hand, as follows. Starting at the top right-hand side, insert the needle from the back, 6mm away from the seam line. Pull the thread through. Insert the needle just behind the pulled-out thread, then bring it out again about 3mm in front (diagram Q). This forms a strong, yet almost invisible stitch. Press and remove tacking stitches.

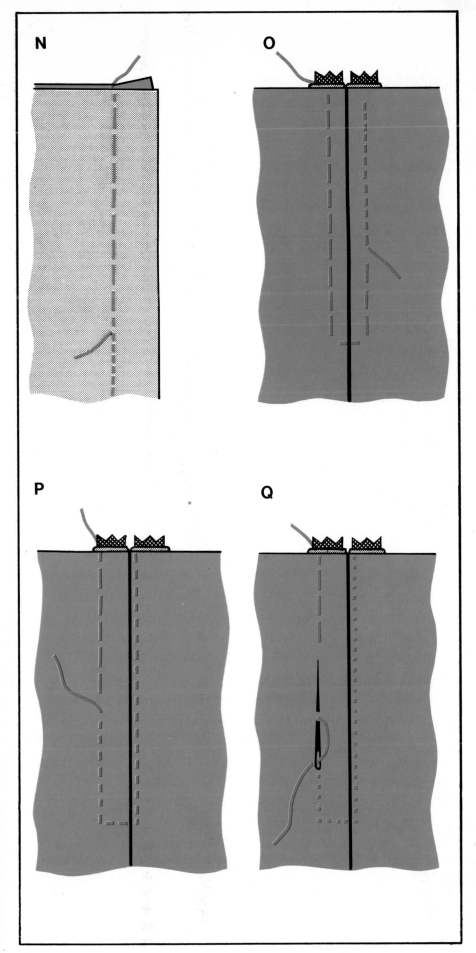

Making a Good Hem

Nothing looks worse than a wavy, lumpy hem, with the impression of stitches and ridges showing on the right side. A garment should have been finished off and well pressed before you start on the hem. Always allow a garment to hang up, at least overnight, before levelling the hem (a flared skirt, or one with any bias cutting, should hang for two days or more), to allow the fabric to drop.

To level the hem you will need a long mirror, pins or tailor's chalk and a yardstick or hem marker. Put on the garment and mark a line around the skirt hem at the chosen distance from the floor, then mark the skirt with an even line of pins or chalk all around. Lay the skirt part flat on a table, right side up. Run a single tacking around, following the pins or chalk marks. Remove pins.

On straight or only slightly-flared skirts, the hem can be up to 7.5cm deep (average is 6cm). Really flared styles should have narrower hems, never more than 2.5cm, otherwise it is difficult to stitch the edge to the garment without making pleats or tucks. Mark and trim the hem allowance evenly, measuring down from the marked turn-up line (diagram R). Turn the hem allowance to the inside, with the tacked marking line along the fold edge, and insert pins to hold. Tack 6mm from the fold edge (diagram S).

Finishing: Neaten the raw edge, either by overcasting closely, by zigzagging, pinking or neatening with bias binding (for fabrics that fray badly). Pin and tack the hem to the garment a second time, now 1cm from the neatened edge, matching seams. Turn back the edge of the hem as far as the tacking will allow, so that you are working beneath it, and blind-stitch in place (diagram T), picking up only a thread from the skirt. Leave each stitch loose: the stitches should be at least 6mm long, so that the hem

Putting in a zip

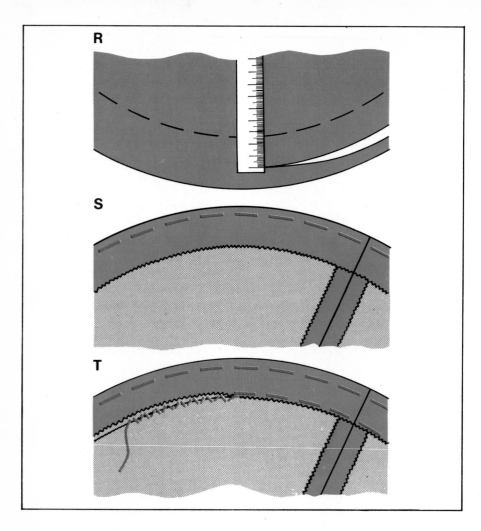

R

S

T

Making a good hem

is not sewn down tightly to the fabric.

Pressing: Lightly press the fold edge only. Remove all tacks and press the hem again, more firmly; if the hem edge has been bound, avoid pressing over the binding, otherwise the impression will show on the right side. Lastly, run the point of the iron along, under the loose edge of the hem, to remove any imprint made by the first pressing.

Flared hems: On really full skirts, trim the hem allowance down to 1cm below the marked line. Turn under the raw edge for 5mm and edge-stitch (avoid stretching the fabric). Trim the excess fabric away to the stitching line, turn under the hem to the marked tack line, and slip-stitch lightly in place. Press carefully, to avoid making a wavy edge.

How to line a dress

Adding a lining to a dress makes it more comfortable to wear, helps it to keep its shape and gives a smooth, neat appearance to the inside, without too much neatening. It is an easy matter to give your dresses this extra-special finish.

To calculate how much 90cm-wide fabric you need to line a plain, fairly straight dress, simply allow twice your normal dress length; if you want to line the sleeves too, just add one sleeve length to the previous amount. If your pattern has a number of seams or a panelled skirt, it is best to lay out the relevant main pattern tissues as if you were placing them on a doubled 90cm-width fabric, then measure the amount needed. Choose a suitable lining fabric for the garment: if your outer material is washable, you must use a washable lining, such as

Tricel taffeta or fine cotton lawn.

To make the lining: Select the main pattern pieces used to make your dress. If there are any pleats in the skirt, fold these flat on the pattern before cutting out, and make the panel into a plain seam. If you have altered the dress in fitting, remember to make the same adjustments to the pattern before cutting out the lining.

Make up the main body part of the lining in the same way as the garment, unless your pattern states otherwise. Where the dress fastens, leave an opening about 1·5cm longer than the dress opening; don't finish off the hem at this stage. Neaten seam edges on the skirt part of the lining. If sleeve linings are to be used, make them up but do not insert them or finish lower edges.

To attach the lining: Turn the finished and well-pressed dress inside out and place the lining over it, wrong sides together. Pull sleeves through the armholes of the lining. Pin the lining to the dress along the shoulder seams and around armholes, pin bust darts of lining and dress together. Make snips 6mm long around the neck edge of the lining, then turn the lining under for 1·5cm and pin to the neck facing, matching seams. Turn under and pin the lining to the zip tape.

Back-stitch the armhole edges together just outside the original seam line. If the sleeves are to be left unlined, overcast the raw edges together; if lined, slip the correct sleeve lining over each dress sleeve, turn under raw edges at the armhole and cuff for 1·5cm and pin, leaving a little ease on the length. Hem the lining to the dress where pinned.

Place the dress on a hanger, still inside out, and mark the lower edge of the lining about 2cm up from the finished edge of the skirt. Turn the lining under, along the marked line, and press. Turn the raw edge under and stitch by hand or machine. Catch the lining to the skirt at side seams, using 2·5cm-long French tacks.

Simply Beautiful

An embroidered dress, inspired by traditional English smocks.

Measurements: To fit 87–92cm bust; finished back length is 114cm.
Materials: 3·7m of 90cm wide fabric; matching thread; interfacing; 40cm zip; 1 skein each of eight toning shades of stranded embroidery cotton.

To cut out: Following our diagram in which one square repre-

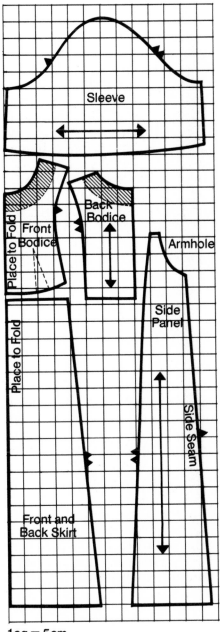

1sq = 5cm

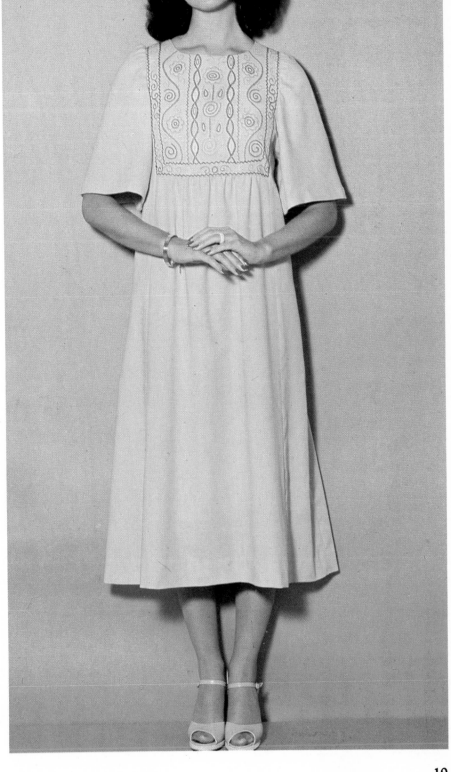

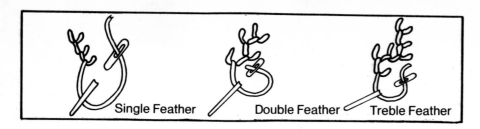

Single Feather   Double Feather   Treble Feather

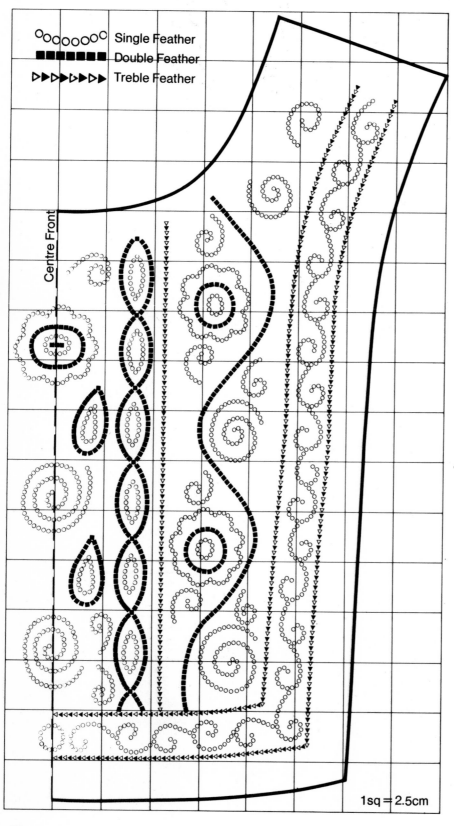

○○○○○○○○ Single Feather
■■■■■■■■ Double Feather
▷▶▷▶▷▶▷▶ Treble Feather

Centre Front

1 sq = 2.5cm

sents 5cm, make a paper pattern for all dress pieces. Trace off shaded areas for front and back neck facings. 1·5cm turnings have been included. Fold fabric in half lengthwise. Place pattern pieces in position to cut sleeve, facings, and front and back bodice, once, and skirt and side panel twice through double thickness of fabric. Make sure front bodice and skirt pieces are placed to fold, and arrows on other pieces are placed to straight grain of fabric. Cut out and mark position of dart and notches.

Embroidery: On wrong side of front bodice make darts and press towards sides. Following stitch diagram, in which one square represents 2·5cm, draw embroidery design on to tracing paper. To complete design, take a tracing of first half, then turn paper over to obtain opposite half of pattern. Join tracings, matching centre front carefully. Pin tracing to bodice and transfer design to fabric. The easiest way to do this is with dressmakers' carbon and a sharp pencil. However, do keep the lines light and clear so that the embroidery will cover them.

Use two of the six strands of cotton for all stitches. Vary the thread colour as desired, and follow the stitch plan to work embroidery. When completed, press the embroidery well on wrong side.

To make: Fold one skirt piece in half lengthwise and cut along fold —this will form the centre back seam. Run two rows of gathering thread across top edge of front and back skirt pieces, 1·5cm and 1cm from raw edges. Draw up gathers evenly to fit lower edges of appropriate bodice piece. With right sides together and edges level, stitch front skirt to front bodice and back skirts to back bodices. Press seams upwards and neaten edges together.

With right sides together, edges level and notches matching, stitch

Examples of single, double and treble feather stitching for embroidered front

the two pairs of side panels together along side seams, press open and neaten edge. With right sides together, edges level and top edge of side panel level with notch on bodice, stitch one edge of side panel to front and other edge to back. Stitch second side panel in place in same way. With right sides together and the edges level, stitch shoulder seams and centre back seam, leaving 41·5cm open for zip. Press seams open, neaten edges; insert zip. Apply inter-

facing to wrong side of neck facing. Stitch facings together across shoulder seams, trim turnings and press open. Neaten outer edge of facing. With right sides together and seams matching, stitch facing around neckline; trim turnings, snip on curves, turn to inside and press seam to edge. Turn under raw edges and catch-stitch to zip tape. Catch-stitch edge of facing to seams. With right sides together, stitch sleeve under-arm seam; press open and neaten edges. Run

gathering thread around sleeve head between notches. Draw up gathers to fit armhole. With right sides together, notches matching and gathers distributed evenly, stitch sleeve into the armhole. Overcast raw edges together. Around lower edges of sleeve, fold 1cm, then 2·5cm to wrong side and blind-stitch in place. Repeat with other sleeve.

Around lower edge of skirt fold 1cm, then 5cm, to wrong side and blind-stitch in place. Press well.

All set for the sun

BIKINI

Measurements: To fit 87–92cm bust, 92–97cm hips.
Materials: 40cm of 150cm wide washable jersey; matching thread; 2m of 6mm wide elastic.

To cut out: Following our diagram, in which one square represents 5cm, make a paper pattern. 1·5cm turnings are included. For larger size follow dotted line where appropriate. Open out fabric and re-fold as shown in diagram, and place pattern in position. Cut out. From remainder of fabric cut two strips 3cm wide by 1m long and one length 3cm by 70cm for ties.

To make: (Use a slight zigzag stitch for seaming, if possible.) With right sides facing, stitch front and back of pants together at sides and along crutch seams. Press seams open. Zigzag-stitch all raw edges to neaten. At top edge turn 2cm to wrong side and machine-stitch in place 5mm from neatened edge, leaving an opening for elastic. Around legs, turn 1·5cm to wrong side and machine 5mm from neatened edge, leaving opening for elastic. Cut elastic 94cm for top and 46cm for each leg. Thread elastic through top edge and legs, adjusting as necessary. Secure ends firmly. Along notched edges of bra pieces fold 5mm then another 5mm to wrong side. Stitch in place. Zigzag-stitch both raw ends to neaten, then turn 1·5cm to wrong side. Stitch across ends 5mm from neatened edges. With right sides together, fold straps in half lengthwise and machine-stitch along length 5mm from edges. Turn to right side and press. Thread the short strip through the narrower side of each bra piece; tie in a bow to form a circle. Thread a long tie through each of the remaining sides. Turn in and slip-stitch all tie ends. One long tie fastens behind neck and other across back.

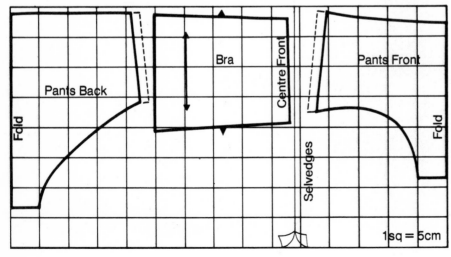

HALTER-NECK SUNDRESS

Measurements: To fit 87–92cm bust; finished back length 79cm.
Materials: 1·10m of 150cm wide washable jersey; matching thread; 30cm zip.

To cut out: Following our diagram, in which one square represents 5cm, make a paper pattern. Follow dotted lines where appropriate for larger size. 1cm turnings have been included. Fold fabric in half widthways and place pattern in position as shown in diagram. Make sure arrows follow straight grain. Cut out. Mark notches and dots on to fabric.

To make: (If possible use a slight zigzag stitch for seaming.) With right sides together and notches matching, stitch fronts to backs along side seams. Neaten and press open. With right side of armhole binding to wrong side of dress, and edges level, stitch binding to back and front armhole, taking a 1·5cm seam. Fold 5mm to wrong side along remaining edge of binding and fold this edge over to right side of garment, so that it is level with previous line of stitching. Top-stitch in place near to fold. Top-stitch a second row along centre of binding. Trim ends level with garment. With one edge of binding level with centre front edge, stitch neck bindings to front necklines in same way, allowing excess binding to protrude at shoulder to form ties. Fold raw edges of tie to wrong side to correspond with binding. Top-stitch two rows along binding and tie in one operation. Run a row of gathers between dots on centre fronts. Pull up gathers to measure 2cm between dots. With right sides together and edges level, stitch centre front seam and centre back seam leaving 30cm open at top of back for zip. Neaten and press seam open. Insert zip. At lower edge fold 5mm then 1·5cm to wrong side. Top-stitch in place and top-stitch second row in centre of hem. Neaten ends of tie if necessary.

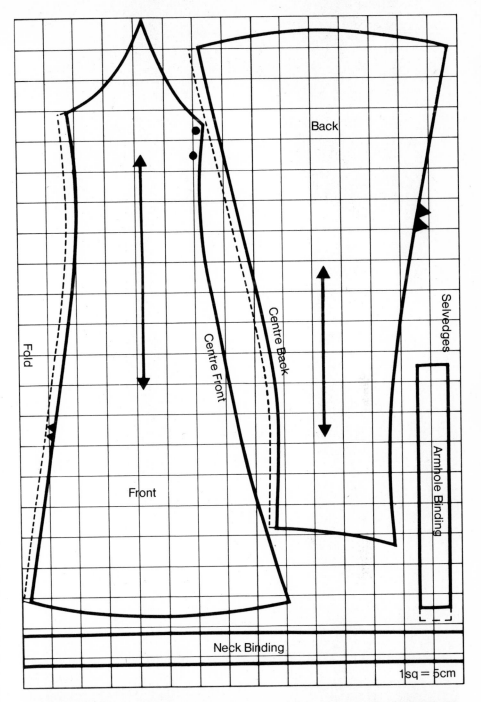

Back

Selvedges

Armhole Binding

Centre Back

Centre Front

Fold

Front

Neck Binding

1 sq = 5cm

24

Playtime partners

Sturdy jeans and shorts for everyday romping around, and for holidays.

Measurements: To fit 51—56cm waist; finished outside leg length— shorts 23cm, trousers, 71cm.
Materials: Shorts — 60cm of 90cm wide fabric; trousers—1·10m of 90cm wide fabric; matching thread; 10cm zip; 60cm of 3cm wide elastic; 1, 13mm button.

To cut out: Following our diagram in which one square represents 5cm, make a paper pattern for trouser piece and pocket. Follow appropriate line across pattern for shorts. 1·5cm turnings, 5cm hems on trousers and 2·5cm hems

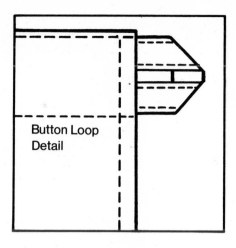

Button Loop Detail

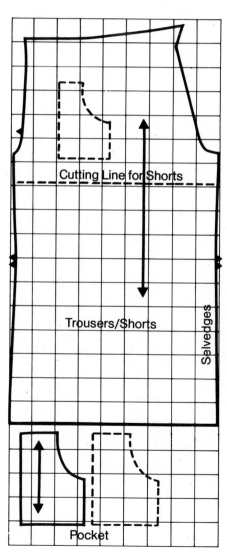

Cutting Line for Shorts

Trousers/Shorts

Selvedges

Pocket

1sq = 5cm

on shorts have been included. Fold fabric in half lengthwise so that selvedges are together at one side. Pin pattern to fabric, as in diagram, and cut out. Cut second pocket as shown on pattern. Mark the notch and pocket positions on the fabric. Cut a strip 3·5cm by 9cm for button loop.

To make: With right sides facing, stitch both pairs of pocket pieces together around edges, leaving an opening at lower edge to turn them through. Trim turnings, snip on curves, and turn pockets through to right side. Press seam to edge and catch-stitch opening closed. Tack pockets to trouser pieces at marked position. Top-stitch pockets in place around all straight edges, then press well. Fold each trouser piece in half with right sides together and double notched edges level. Stitch along double notched seams to form two separate legs. Press seams open and neaten raw edges. With right sides facing, insert one 'leg' inside the other. Then, with right sides facing and edges level, stitch legs together around crutch seam from top of centre back to notch on centre front. Press seam open and neaten raw edges. Insert zip in centre front seam immediately above notch. Tack turning to the wrong side along remaining centre front seam above zip. Neaten raw edge around waist. Fold 5cm to the wrong side around waist edge

and stitch in place 4cm from the fold. Stitch again near to the fold to complete casing.

Fold 5mm to the wrong side along long edges of button loop. Fold in half lengthwise so that folded edges are level, and top-stitch along both long edges. Fold strip to form a mitred loop, as shown at left, and insert raw ends at appropriate end of casing. Tack in place to one side of casing only. Insert elastic through casing and pull up. At each end of casing, stitch through casing and elastic to secure ends of elastic and loop. Neaten lower edge of each leg, fold hem to wrong side and blind-stitch.

There is a large and varied selection of appliqué motifs available which make decorative additions to children's clothes. The patch shown below is just one possibility.

An exotic evening kaftan

Measurements: To fit 87–92cm bust; finished back length—148cm.
Materials: 3·10m of 115cm wide fabric; matching thread; 8m of 1·5cm wide ribbon; 16, 1cm buttons; thread for button loops; 30cm of 90cm wide interfacing.

To cut out: Following our diagram in which one square represents 5cm, make a paper pattern for all pieces. Trace off shaded areas on front and back to make neck facings. 1·5cm turnings and 5cm hems have been included. Fold fabric in half lengthwise, and place pattern as shown in diagram. Make sure back and back neck facing are to the fold, and that arrows follow the straight grain of the fabric. Cut out. Mark position of darts, dots and notches on fabric. Fold collar pattern in half lengthwise and from interfacing cut half collar depth. Cut a pair of front facings from interfacing.

To make: Stitch darts on wrong side of fronts, and press. With right sides together and edges level, stitch centre front seam below notch only, and front to back along shoulder seams. Press seams open and neaten edges. With right sides together and edges level, place top of sleeve to armhole edge so that dot on sleeve matches shoulder seam and double notches match. Stitch to armhole. Press seams open and neaten edges. With right sides together and edges level, stitch under-arm sleeve seams and side seams above dots in one operation. Press seams open and neaten raw edges along complete length. Apply interfacing to wrong side of front facings and half of collar. With right sides meeting, stitch centre front seam of front facings together below notch. Stitch front facing to back facing across shoulders. Trim facing seams and press open. Neaten outer edge of facing. With right sides together, stitch one long edge of collar around neckline of dress and other long edge around neck edge of the facing. Trim turnings, snip curves, press seams open. Fold half of collar and facings over to the outside of the garment so that neck seams match and centre front edges of facing and dress are level. Stitch collar together along short edges, and front facing to dress along opening. Trim turnings and turn collar right side out. Fold facings to inside of garment and press seams to the edge. Tack neck and front facing in position. Neaten around lower edge of sleeves and skirt. Fold 5cm hems to the wrong side and tack in place. Try on and adjust length, if necessary. Catch-stitch hems in position. Fold and tack 5cm to the wrong side along either side of the skirt slits.

To trim: Tack first row of ribbon around lower edge of sleeves 1cm from edge, turning ends under to neaten. Tack a second row of ribbon around sleeve 1cm above the first row. Top-stitch in place along both edges of ribbon. In the same way, top-stitch ribbon around centre front opening and side slits, mitring the corners to form a point. Stitch a row of ribbon along top edge and lower edge of collar so that outer edges of ribbon are level with edges of collar. Remove tacks. Catch-stitch facing to turning on shoulder seams. Stitch buttons to left centre front 2·5cm apart. Work thread loops on right front edge.

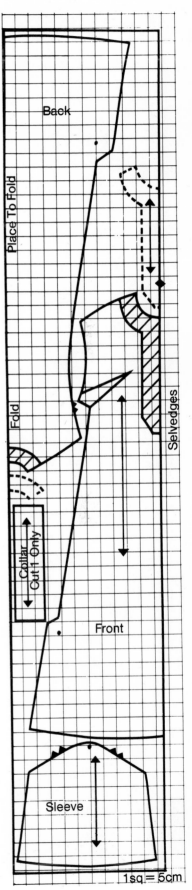

1 sq = 5cm

A touch of class

Materials: 2·5m fabric, 115cm wide; matching thread.
Size: To fit 83–92cm bust. Finished length 98cm.

To cut out: Make a paper pattern following our diagram, in which one square represents 5cm. 1·5cm turnings have been allowed unless otherwise stated. To obtain front and back neck facings, mark in and trace off shaded portions—cutting positions on diagram are indicated by dotted lines. Place pattern pieces as shown on diagram, pin and cut out. Mark pocket positions and centre back line with tailor tacks.

To make: With right sides together and matching notches, stitch front to back at side seams. Trim seams to 5mm, press both edges of seams towards back of garment. Neaten by overcasting or by zigzagging the raw edges together.

Sleeve bands: With right sides meeting, join short ends of each sleeve band to form two rings. Place over lower edges of sleeves, right sides together, bottom raw edges level, and seams matching at the underarm. Pin, tack and stitch band in place taking 5mm turnings. Press edges towards band. Fold band to inside; turn raw edge under for 5mm and hem in place to previous line of stitching. Press bands.

Pockets: Place pockets right sides together, in two pairs; stitch around edges, leaving about 5cm open. Trim turnings and corners then turn through openings to the right side. Tack edges, pulling out seam with the point of needle as you go to make square corners. Slip-stitch opening together. Press. Remove tacks. Place pockets on outside of kimono fronts at marked positions, pin, tack and edge-stitch in place along sides of pockets. Fasten off threads firmly at corners. Remove tacks and press.

On the pattern diagram (left):

- Cut 2 (Sleeve Bands)
- Back Facing / Cut 1
- Back
- Cut 1 To Fold
- Fold
- Front / Cut 2
- Selvedges
- Pocket Position
- Tie Belt
- Front Facing
- Pocket / Cut 2
- Pocket / Cut 2

1 sq = 5 cm

Front bands (these are formed by stitching facings on to the outside): With right sides together and matching notches, join front facings to back neck facing at shoulders. Press seams open. Turn kimono to the wrong side and with wrong side of facing uppermost place raw edges together. Taking 5mm turnings and matching centre back lines and shoulder seams of kimono and facing, pin and stitch facing in position. Snip around back neck curve, turn facing over to the outside of garment and tack edge through all thicknesses, pulling out stitched seam with the needle's point as you go. Turn opposite raw edge of facing under for 5mm, pin and tack in place, keeping an even width all round (to match sleeve bands). Edge-stitch both edges of facing to hold in position. Stitch sleeve bands on both edges in the same way.

Tie belt: With right sides together join two belt strips together across two short ends. Press seam open. Fold in half lengthwise, right sides together, and stitch across short ends and along one long edge, leaving about 5cm open. Trim corners and turn through to right side. Tack edges. Sew up opening and press. Remove tacks and press again if necessary. Try on kimono, tie belt in place and mark position for belt carriers at side seams. Check length. Trim lower edge and overcast or zigzag. Turn hem under for 4cm or amount required. Tack and blindstitch in place. Press. Make thread or rouleau belt carriers from spare fabric and attach.

Detail of pocket and tie belt

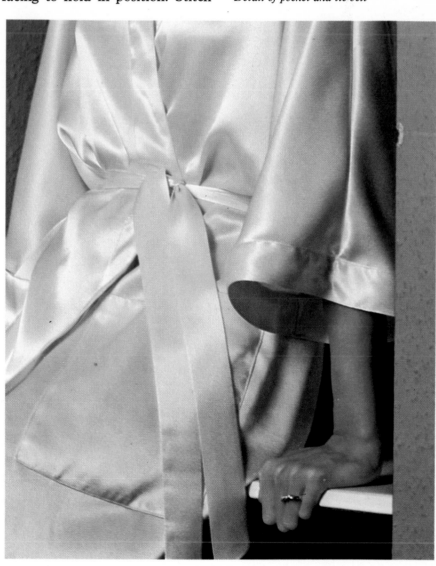

True blue

Here's a beautiful kaftan with a face-framing hood that will protect you from the rays of the noonday sun. It's perfect for drifting and dreaming—and very easy to sew.

Size To fit 87–92cm bust; finished back length 150cm.
Materials: 4·5m of 90cm wide fabric; matching thread. 1·5cm seams allowed; 5cm hem.

To cut out: Following our diagram, in which one square represents 5cm, make a paper pattern for main dress piece (front and back alike), sleeve and hood. Mark end of tucks and lower dotted neckline on to pattern. Open fabric out to full width and, beginning at one end, place pattern on to fabric as shown in diagram, making sure enough fabric remains at end to cut another dress piece. Cut out.

Remove dress pattern, trim along lower dotted neckline to make front. Replace pattern on fabric and cut out the front. Mark end of line of tucks on fabric. Cut one strip 150cm by 3cm and one 40cm by 3cm.

To make: Fold front and back in half lengthwise and mark centre fold with single tack line. With wrong sides together form and stitch six tucks, each 1cm deep either side of the centre line on front and back, beginning at top edge and finishing level with the marked line. Make the first two tucks 1·5cm either side of centre tacked line. Working towards side edge, make subsequent tucks 3cm apart. Press tucks flat towards side seams.

Cut along centre front fold line for 18cm from neck edge to make opening. Bind around opening continuously, using the shorter strip.

With right sides together, edges level and tucks matching, stitch shoulder seams and press open. On sleeves, fold and tack seam

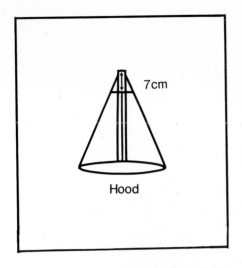

7cm

Hood

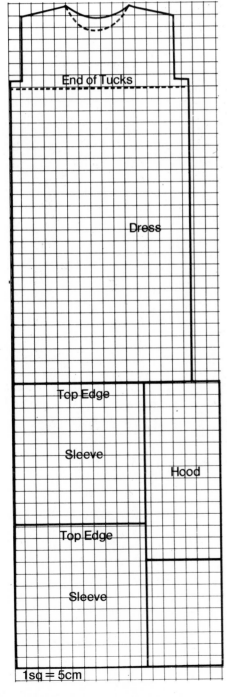

End of Tucks

Dress

Top Edge

Sleeve

Hood

Top Edge

Sleeve

1 sq = 5cm

allowance to the wrong side along top edges and down adjacent side edges for 6cm. Lay out front and back of dress so armhole is flat and the right side uppermost.

Place turned top edge of sleeve on to armhole so edges of turnings are level, and top-stitch in place. With right sides together and edges level, stitch side seams and under-arm sleeve seams. Press seams open.

With right sides together, fold hood in half widthwise and stitch along one edge adjacent to the fold to form back seam. With right sides together, open out hood and refold to form a triangle with the seam running from the point to centre of opposite long edge, as shown in diagram.

Stitch straight across pointed end, 7cm away from point, and trim excess away. Fold 1cm, then 4cm, to the right side across long unseamed edge of hood and stitch in place to form hem.

Run a gathering thread around lower edge of hood. With right sides together and edges level, place lower edge of hood to neck edge. Making sure that hood seam matches centre back, and that front edges are level, pull up gathers to fit neckline and stitch in place. Then trim the turning to 5mm.

With centre of long strip to centre back of neckline, bind neck turnings to neaten, allowing ends to protrude to form ties.

Fold in raw edges of ties and stitch folded edges together; neaten ends by tucking in and stitching.

Adjust length if necessary. At lower edge of sleeves, fold 5mm, then 1·5cm, to wrong side and stitch in place to form hems.

At lower edge of skirt, fold 1cm, then 4cm, to the wrong side and stitch in place.

Detail showing soft, elegant hood and gentle lines of front

Knitting

Basic stitches

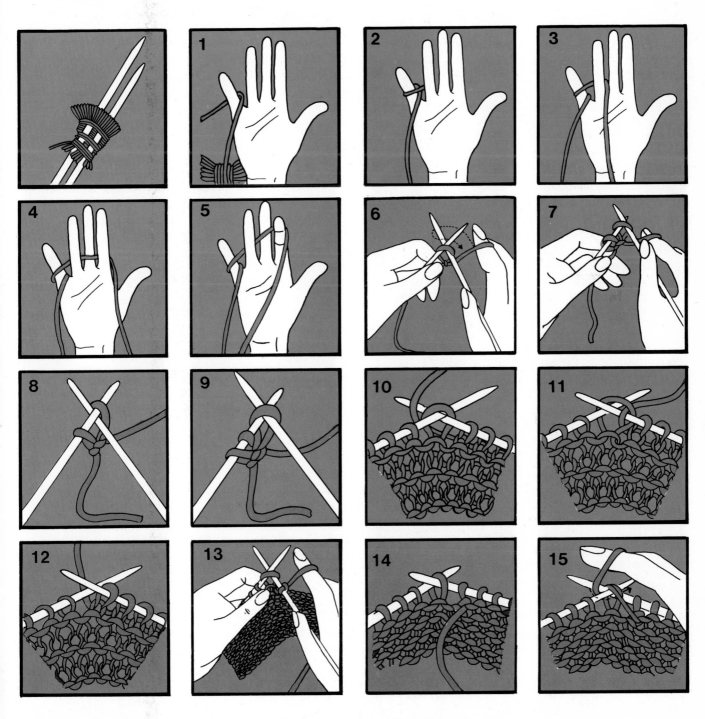

Holding the yarn: There are many different ways of holding yarn and knitting needles, but we have given the one we think is the simplest. The important thing is to develop a style that you find comfortable. Wind yarn around the little finger of your right hand (sketches 1 and 2), across the back of the third finger and the front of the second finger (sketches 3 and 4). Finally wind yarn around back

Step-by-step knitting

of forefinger (sketch 5). Practise this a few times. You are now ready to cast on.

Casting on: First make a slip

loop and place on left-hand needle. Wind yarn around the fingers of the right hand as practised. Put point of right-hand needle through front of loop and, holding the needles as shown (sketch 6), wind yarn around right-hand needle and draw the yarn and point of right-hand needle back through the original loop, then transfer the second (new) loop to left-hand needle (sketch 7) and draw point of right-hand needle out. ⋆ Insert right-hand needle between the last 2 stitches on left-hand needle (sketch 8), wind yarn around point of right-hand needle, draw the yarn and point of right-hand needle through to right side thus making another loop; transfer this loop to left-hand needle (sketch 9) and draw right-hand needle out. Repeat from ⋆ until you have the number of stitches that you require. You are now ready to start knitting.

To work a 'knit' stitch: Taking the needle holding the cast-on stitches in your left hand and keeping the yarn at back of work, ⋆ put point of right-hand needle through front of first stitch on left-hand needle and, using index finger, put yarn under point of right-hand needle and then over this needle, keeping yarn under point of left-hand needle. Pull point of right-hand needle through the original stitch, keeping the stitch just made on the right-hand needle and slipping the old stitch off left-hand needle so that it drops down a row (sketches 10, 11 and 12). Repeat from ⋆ to end of row. If you knit every stitch on every row, this forms a fabric called garter-stitch. When counting rows in garter-stitch, each ridge on one side of your knitting represents two rows worked. Practise this stitch for a few rows. If you knit 20 rows you will have 10 ridges on each side of your work. Now you are ready to cast off.

Casting off: To cast off a knit row, knit the first two stitches on to the right-hand needle, ⋆ then put point of left-hand needle through first stitch on right-hand

needle and lift this stitch over the second stitch; slip it off both needles (sketch 13). Knit next stitch from left-hand needle on to right-hand needle so that you again have 2 stitches on right-hand needle. Now repeat from ⋆ until all stitches have been knitted from left-hand needle and you have one stitch remaining on right-hand needle. Cut yarn, and thread the end through the remaining stitch. Slip stitch off right-hand needle and firmly draw up end of yarn to secure the last stitch.

To knit two stitches together: Instead of putting the point of right-hand needle through the front of the first stitch on left-hand needle, put the point through the front of second stitch on left-hand needle and then through the front of the first stitch so that you have caught up two stitches with the point of right-hand needle. Wind yarn around right-hand needle and draw the yarn and point of right-hand needle back through the original two loops, drawing point of left-hand needle out of the original two stitches. You have now decreased by one stitch.

In knitting there are only two basic stitches—knit and purl. All patterns use one or other of these stitches or, in most cases, a combination of both. Once you know how to do both, you will be able to work in stocking-stitch, the smoothest of all knitted fabrics. Also, by alternating a number of knit stitches with a number of purl stitches on the same row, you will be able to work a variety of ribs.

To work a purl stitch: Take the needle holding the stitches in your left hand and the other needle in your right hand. Insert the point of right-hand needle from back to front (sketch 14). Keeping the yarn at the front of the work, pass the yarn over the top of right-hand needle and around point of needle in an anti-clockwise direction (sketch 15) thus making a loop. Draw this loop through the stitch on left-hand needle, thus forming

a new stitch on right-hand needle and slipping the old stitch off left-hand needle so that it drops down a row. Repeat from ⋆ to end of row. If you knit one row and purl one row alternately, you will have stocking-stitch when the smooth side is facing you; reversed stocking-stitch when the ridged side is facing you.

When changing from a knit stitch to a purl stitch in the middle of a row, bring the yarn from the back of the work between the points of the needles to the front, ready to purl the next stitch. When changing from a purl stitch to a knit stitch, pass the yarn from the front of the work between the points of the needles to the back, ready to knit the next stitch. The more you practise these stitches, the more even your work will gradually become.

To make buttonholes: There are various methods of working buttonholes, and each pattern gives exact instructions on how and where to work them. The two below, however, are the most widely used.

By the first method, buttonholes can be worked either in the main body of the front or on a buttonhole band which is usually knitted separately then sewn on. On the first buttonhole row a given number of stitches are cast off a few stitches from the front edge. On the second buttonhole row the same number of stitches are cast on above those cast off, thus completing the buttonhole.

The second method is used where only a small buttonhole is required—for example, on garments for babies. It is completed on one row and usually worked as follows: yarn forward, K 2 together, pattern to end.

Hat and scarf

Materials: Emu Superwash Double Knitting. **Scarf:** 10 (25g) balls. **Hat:** 4 (25g) balls. For best results it is essential to use recommended yarn. Pair 4½mm knitting needles.

Measurements: The scarf will measure 158cm in length and 19cm in width. The hat will fit an average size head.

Tension: 19 sts to 10cm in width over the garter-st. Cast on 19 sts and K 20 rows. If your knitting measures less than 10cm you are working at too tight a tension—change to a larger needle. If your work measures more than 10cm you are working at too loose a tension—change to a smaller needle. It is essential that you work at the tension recommended, so, if necessary, experiment with different size needles until you achieve the correct tension.

Abbreviations: K—knit plain; st(s) — stitch(es); cm — centimetres; garter-st is K plain on every row.

SCARF

Cast on 37 sts and work 194cm in garter-st. Cast off. Turn up 18cm at each end for pockets and back-stitch the side seams. Turn to right side and press seams lightly.

HAT

Cast on 91 sts and work 80 rows in garter-st. **To shape crown:** *1st dec row:* * K 7, K 2 tog; repeat from * until 1 st remains, K 1. 81 sts. K 3 rows. *2nd dec row:* * K 6, K 2 tog; repeat from * until 1 st remains, K 1. 71 sts. K 3 rows. *3rd dec row:* * K 5, K 2 tog; repeat from * until 1 st remains, K 1. 61 sts. K 3 rows. *4th dec row:* * K 4, K 2 tog; repeat from * until 1 st remains, K 1. 51 sts. K 3 rows. *5th dec row:* * K 3, K 2 tog; repeat from * until 1 st remains, K 1. 41 sts. K 3 rows. *6th dec row:* * K 2, K 2 tog; repeat from * until 1 st remains, K 1. 31 sts. K 3 rows. *7th dec row:* * K 1, K 2 tog; repeat from * until 1 st remains, K 1. 21 sts. K 1 row. *8th dec row:* * K 2 tog; repeat from * until 1 st remains, K 1. 11 sts. K 1 row. Break off yarn leaving an end long enough to join the side seam. Thread this end through remain-

ing 11 sts and draw up tightly. Secure with a back-st. Now with the wrong side of work facing you back-stitch the seam to within 15cm of cast-on-edge. Turn the hat to the right side and back-stitch the remainder of the seam. Press seam lightly. Turn back brim.

Jiffy jackets

Abbreviations: K—knit plain; st(s) — stitch(es); cm — centimetres; garter-st is K plain on every row.

To work the back: Begin at the lower edge by casting on 62 (66, 70, 74) sts. Work straight in garter-st—the first row will be on the wrong side of work—until work measures 51 (53, 55, 57)cm. Cast off.

Left front: Begin at lower edge by casting on 31 (33, 35, 37) sts and work straight in garter-st—the first row will be on the wrong side of work—until work measures 47 (49, 51, 53)cm ending at the front edge—you will have worked an even number of rows. **To shape neck:** Cast off 10 sts at the beginning of the next row then K to end. 21 (23, 25, 27) sts. Continue straight in garter-st on these sts until work measures same as the back. Cast off.

Right front: Begin at lower edge by casting on 31 (33, 35, 27) sts and work straight in garter-st—the first row will be on the wrong side of work—until work measures 47 (49, 51, 53)cm ending at the front edge—you will have worked an uneven number of rows. **To shape neck:** Cast off 10 sts at the beginning of the next row then K to end. 21 (23, 25, 27) sts. Continue straight in garter-st on these sts until work measures the same as the back. Cast off.

To make up: Press all pieces very lightly using a warm iron over a damp cloth. Join shoulder seams, then join side seams leaving 19 (19, 20, 20)cm open for armholes. Lightly press seams.

Ties (make 2): Using 2 strands of yarn each 76cm long, make a twisted cord and knot the end. Thread folded end through knitting at neck edge, open up the folded end and thread the knotted end through the folded end. Draw up tightly to secure cord in position.

Materials: 6 (7, 7, 8) 50g balls Patons Capstan. For best results it is essential to use recommended yarn. Pair 5½mm knitting needles.

Measurements: To fit 76 (82, 87, 92)cm bust; length—51 (53, 55, 57)cm. The figures in brackets refer to the larger sizes. Underline the figures referring to the size you are going to make.

Tension: 15 sts to 10cm in width over the garter-st. Cast on 15sts and K 20 rows. If your knitting measures less than 10 cm you are working at too tight a tension—change to a larger needle. If your work measures more than 10cm you are working at too loose a tension—change to a smaller needle. It is essential that you work at the tension recommended, so, if necessary, experiment with different size needles until you achieve the correct tension.

Aran Sweaters

Materials: 20 (21, 22, 23, 24, 25) 50g balls Gaelic Bainin by 3 Suisses. For best results, it is essential to use recommended yarn. For all sizes, a pair each of 4½mm, 3¾mm and 3¼mm needles; 2 cable needles.

Measurements:

Woman's sweater: To fit 87 (92, 97)cm bust. Length—68·5 (69, 70)cm. Sleeve seam—47 (48, 48·5)cm.

Man's sweater: To fit 102 (107, 112)cm chest. Length—72 (73, 74)cm. Sleeve seam—49·5 (50, 51)cm. Figures in brackets refer to larger sizes.

Note: The 87 (92, 97)cm sizes are for women's tunic-length sweaters with patterned collars; the 102 (107, 112)cm sizes are for men's sweaters with crew necks·

Tension: 10 sts to 5cm in width over Irish moss-st, using 4½mm needles.

Abbreviations; K—knit; P—purl; st(s)—stitches; cm—centimetres; tog—together; inc—increase, by working into the front and back of same st; dec—decrease, by working 2 sts tog; IMS—Irish moss-st; YF—yarn forward, bring yarn to front of needle and over it before knitting next st, thus making a st; TW 3—twist 3: slip 1 knitwise, K 1, YF, K 1, then pass slipped st over last 3 sts and off needle; C 6L—cable 6 left: slip next 2 sts on to cable needle, leave at front, slip next 2 sts on to second cable needle and leave at back, K 2, then P 2 from back needle and K 2 from front needle; C 6R—cable 6 right: slip next 4 sts on to cable needle and leave at back. K 2, then slip 2 'P' sts from cable needle back on to left-hand needle, bring cable needle to front, P 2 from left-hand needle and finally K 2 from cable needle.

Back: Using 3¾mm needles, cast on 110 (114, 118, 118, 122, 126) sts. Beginning with 1st (2nd, 1st, 1st, 2nd, 1st) rib row, work 11 (11, 11, 13, 13, 13) rows in rib, as follows: *1st rib row:* K 2, * P 2, K 2; repeat from * to end. *2nd rib row:* P 2, * K 2, P 2; repeat from * to end. **Note:** It is essential to begin with correct rib row given for size

you are making. *Inc row (wrong side):* * Inc, rib 1 (1, 2, 2, 2, 2); repeat from * 4 times, inc, rib 1 (3, 0, 0, 2, 0) *, ** P 2, K 2; repeat from ** 6 times, P 2, *** K 2, inc purlwise, P 1; repeat from *** 5 (5, 5, 5, 5, 7) times, **** K 2, P 2; repeat from **** 7 times, then repeat from * to *. 128 (132, 136, 136, 140, 146) sts. Change to 4½mm needles and work in pattern, as follows: *1st row:* For IMS * K 1, P 1; repeat from * 8 (9, 10, 10, 11, 10) times, for cable panel ** K 2, P 2; repeat from ** 6 times, K 2, for centre panel *** P 2, TW 3, P 2, K 3; repeat from *** twice (twice, twice, twice, twice, 3 times), P 2, for cable panel **** K 2, P 2; repeat from **** 6 times, K 2, then for IMS P 1 and K 1 alternately to end. In all cases, ribs for cable panels will continue straight up from welt. *2nd row:* * P 1, K 1; repeat from * 8 (9, 10, 10, 11, 10) times, rib 30, ** K 2, P 3; repeat from ** 5 (5, 5, 5, 5, 7) times, K 2, rib 30, then K 1 and P 1 alternately to end. *3rd row:* * P 1, K 1; repeat from * 7 (8, 9, 9, 10, 9) times, P 2, rib 30, ** P 2, K 3, P 2, TW3; repeat from ** twice (twice, twice, twice, twice, 3 times), P 2, rib 30, P 2, then K 1 and P 1 alternately to end. *4th row:* * K 1, P 1; repeat from * 7 (8, 9, 9, 10, 9) times, K 2, rib 30, ** K 2, P 3; repeat from ** 5 (5, 5, 5, 5, 7) times, K 2, rib 30, K 2 then P 1 and K 1 alternately to end. *5th row:* Work 18 (20, 22, 22, 24, 22) sts in IMS, as set on 1st row, * C 6L, P 2; repeat from * twice, C 6L, work over centre panel as on 1st row, ** C 6L, P 2; repeat from ** twice, C 6L, work in IMS to end as on 1st row. *6th row:* As 2nd row. *7th row:* As 3rd row. *8th row:* As 4th row. *9th row:* As 1st row. *10th row:* As 2nd row. *11th row:* Work 18 (20, 22, 22, 24, 22) sts in IMS as on 3rd row, K 2, P 2, * C 6R, P 2; repeat from * twice, K 2, work over centre panel as on 3rd row, K 2, P 2, ** C 6R, P 2; repeat from ** twice, K 2, then K 1 and P 1 alternately to end. *12th row:* As 4th row. These 11 rows form pattern. **Woman's sweater only:**

Continuing in pattern, dec 1 st at both ends of next row and 5 following 8th rows, then continue straight until work measures 35·5 cm from cast-on edge. Inc 1 st at both ends of next row and 2 following 12th rows. Continue straight until work measures 49·5 (49·5, 49·5)cm from cast-on edge, ending with a wrong-side row. **Man's sweater only:** Continue straight in pattern until work measures 51 (51, 51)cm from cast-on edge, ending with a wrong-side row. Now continue *for all sizes.* 122 (126, 130, 136, 140, 146) sts. **To shape armholes:** Cast off 7 sts at beginning of next 2 rows and 6 (7, 8, 5, 6, 7) sts at beginning of following 2 rows. 96 (98, 100, 112, 114, 118) sts. Continue straight until armholes measure 17 (18, 18·5, 19·5, 20, 21)cm, ending with a wrong-side row. *Now divide sts for neck and shoulders. Next row:* Pattern 38 (39, 40, 46, 47, 48) and slip these sts on to spare needle, cast off next 20 (20, 20, 20, 20, 22) sts, pattern to end and work on these last 38 (39, 40, 46, 47, 48) sts. **Left back shoulder:** Work 1 row straight—work 2 rows here on right back shoulder—then cast off 4 sts at beginning of next row and following alternate row. **To slope shoulder:** Cast off 8 sts at beginning of next row and 3 (3, 3, 2, 2, 2) sts at neck edge on following row. Repeat last 2 rows once (once, once, twice, twice, twice). Cast off remaining 8 (9, 10, 8, 9, 10) sts. With wrong side of work facing, rejoin wool to neck edge of remaining sts. **Right back shoulder:** Work as for left back shoulder, working extra row where indicated.

Front: Work as for back until armholes measure 12 (13, 13·5, 14·5, 15, 16)cm ending with a wrong-side row. *Now divide sts for neck and shoulders. Next row:* Pattern 39 (40, 41, 47, 48, 49) and slip these sts on to spare needle, cast off next 18 (18, 18, 18, 18, 20) sts, pattern to end and work on these last 39 (40, 41, 47, 48, 49) sts. **Right front shoulder:** Work 1 row straight—work 2 rows here on left front shoulder—then cast off 4 sts at beginning of next row and following alternate row. Dec 1 st at neck edge on following 4 rows. Work 1 row straight, then dec 1 st at neck edge on next row and 2 following alternate rows. **To slope shoulder:** Cast off 8 sts at beginning of next row, then work 1 row straight. Repeat last 2 rows once (once, once, twice, twice, twice). Cast off remaining 8 (9, 10, 8, 9, 10) sts. With wrong side of work facing, rejoin wool to neck edge of remaining sts. **Left front shoulder:** Work as for right front shoulder, working 1 row extra where indicated.

Sleeves (both alike): Using 3¾mm needles, cast on 46 (46, 50, 54, 54, 58) sts. Beginning with 1st (1st, 2nd, 1st, 1st, 2nd) rib row, work 11 (11, 11, 13, 13, 13) rows in rib, as set at beginning of back. *Inc row (wrong side):* ★ Rib 1, inc; repeat from ★ 3 (3, 3, 5, 5, 5) times, rib 0 (0, 2, 0, 0, 2) ★, ★★ P 2, K 2; repeat from ★★ 6 times, P 2, finally repeat from ★ to ★. 54 (54, 58, 66, 66, 70) sts. Change to 4½mm needles and work in pattern, as follows: *1st row:* For IMS ★ K 1, P 1; repeat from ★ 5 (5, 6, 8, 8, 9) times, for cable panel ★★ K 2, P 2; repeat from ★★ 6 times, K 2, then for IMS P 1 and K 1 alternately to end. This row sets pattern for sleeves. Continue in pattern, working side panels in IMS and centre panel of 30 sts in cable for a further 5 rows. Continuing in pattern, inc 1 st at both ends of next row and every following 6th row until there are 86 (88, 92, 98, 100, 104) sts, working extra sts in IMS. Continue straight in pattern until sleeve measures 47 (48, 48·5, 49·5, 50, 51)cm, ending with a wrong-side row. Place a marker at both ends of last row to mark beginning of *Sleeve top.* Work 16 (17, 18, 14, 16, 17) rows straight. Cast off 4 sts at beginning of next 6 (6, 6, 4, 4, 4) rows and 6 sts at beginning of following 4 rows. Cast off 8 sts at beginning of next 2 (2, 2, 4, 4, 4) rows, then cast off remaining sts.
Woman's patterned collar: Using 4½mm needles, cast on 114

sts. *1st row:* P 2, ★ K 2, P 2; repeat from ★ to end. *2nd row:* K 2, ★ inc purlwise, P 1, K 2; repeat from ★ to end. 142 sts. *3rd row:* P 2, ★ TW 3, P 2, K 3, P 2; repeat from ★ to end. *4th row:* K 2, ★ P 3, K 2; repeat from ★ to end. *5th row:* P 2, ★ K 3, P 2, TW 3, P 2; repeat from ★ to end. *6th row:* As 4th row. *7th to 20th rows:* Repeat 3rd to 6th rows 3 times and 3rd and 4th rows again. *21st row:* P 2, ★ K 3, P 2, slip 1 knitwise, K 2, pass slipped st over, P 2; repeat from ★ to end. *22nd row:* K 2, ★ P 2, K 2, P 3, K 2; repeat from ★ to end. *23rd row:* P 2, ★ slip 1 knitwise, K 2, pass slipped st over, P 2, K 2, P 2; repeat from ★ to end. Beginning with 1st rib row, as set on back, work 8 rows in rib. Cast off.

Man's crew neck: Using 3¾mm needles, cast on 126 (126, 130) sts. Beginning with 1st rib row, as set on back, work 7 rows in rib. Change

to 3¼mm needles and rib a further 12 rows. Change back to 3¾mm needles and rib 7 rows. Cast off loosely in rib.

To make up: Do not press. Join shoulder seams. Set in sleeves, matching markers on sleeves to beginning of armhole shaping on main parts. Press seams lightly. Join side and sleeve seams. For crew neck version, join row ends. Right sides together, join cast-on edge of crew neckband to neck edge of sweater. Fold band in half and catch down cast-off edge of band to inside neck edge. For polo collar version, join row ends of collar. With right side of collar to wrong side of sweater and with seam on collar at centre-back neck edge, sew cast-off edge of collar around neck edge. Turn collar to right side.

Detail of neck and front stitching

Baby's first outfit

Materials: Emu Treasure 3-ply. **Matinee coat**: 3 (4) 20g balls. **Bonnet**: 1 ball. **Bootees**: 1 ball. **Mitts**: 1 ball. **Shawl**: 19 balls. For best results it is essential to use recommended yarn. Pair each 3¼mm and 3mm needles; pair extra long 3mm needles for yoke of coat and 3¼mm needles for shawl; medium-sized crochet hook; 3 buttons; 1m of 2·5cm ribbon for bonnet, narrow ribbon for coat, bootees and mitts.

Measurements:
Coat: To fit 46 (48)cm chest; length – 23cm; sleeve seam – 14cm. **Bonnet**: Around face edge—27 (29)cm; face edge to crown—14 (15)cm. **Bootees**: Back of heel to toe—10 (11)cm. **Mitts**: Around hand—11 (12)cm. **Shawl**: 123cm square. Figures in brackets refer to larger size.

Tension: 15 sts to 5cm in width over st-st, using 3¼mm needles.

Abbreviations: K—knit; P—purl; st(s)—stitch(es); cm—centimetres; tog—together; inc—increase, by working into front and back of same st; dec—decrease, by working 2 sts tog; sl—slip; st-st—stocking-st, K on right side and P back; g-st—garter-st, K every row; PSSO—pass slipped st over; YF—yarn forward, to make 1st; TBL—through back of loop(s); DC—double crochet.

COAT

Back: Using a pair of 3¼mm needles, cast on 93 (101) sts and beginning with a K row, work 4 rows in st-st. *Picot row*: K 2, * YF, K 2 tog; repeat from * until 1 st remains, K 1. Beginning with a P row, work 5 rows in st-st. Now work in pattern, as follows. *1st row (right side)*: P. *2nd and following 5 alternate rows*: P. *3rd row*: K 1, * YF, sl 1, K 2 tog, PSSO, YF, K 1; repeat from * to end. *5th row*: K 1, * YF, sl 1, K 2 tog, PSSO, YF, K 5; repeat from * ending last repeat K 1. *7th row*: as 5th row. *9th row*: K 4, * YF, sl 1, K 1, PSSO, K 1, K 2 tog, YF, K 3; repeat from * until 1 st remains, K 1. *11th row*: as 3rd row. *13th row*: P. *14th to 20th rows*: beginning with a P row, work 7 rows in st-st. These 20 rows form pattern. Repeat them once and work first 13 rows again. Mark both ends of row. Beginning with a P row, work 5 rows in st-st. Slip sts on to a spare needle.

Left front: Using a pair of 3¼mm needles, cast on 58 (66) sts and beginning with a K row, work 4 rows in st-st. *Picot row*: K 2, * YF, K 2 tog; repeat from * until 2 sts remain, K 2. Beginning with a P row, work 4 rows in st-st. *Next row*: K 5, P to end. Now work in pattern with g-st border, as follows. *1st row*: P until 5 sts remain, K 5. *2nd and following 5 alternate rows*: K 5, P to end. *3rd row*: K 1, * YF, sl 1, K 2 tog, PSSO, YF, K 1; repeat from * until 5 sts remain, K 5. *5th and 7th rows*: K 1, * YF, sl 1, K 1, PSSO, YF, K 5; repeat from * until 1 st remains, K 1. *9th row*: K 4, * YF, sl 1, K 1, PSSO, K 1, K 2 tog, YF, K 3; repeat from * until 6 sts remain, K 6. *11th row*: as 3rd row. *13th row*: as 1st row. *14th to 20th rows*: beginning with a P row and keeping 5 sts in g-st, work 7 rows in st-st. ** Repeat these 20 rows once and first 13 rows again. Mark side-seam edge of last row. Maintaining border and beginning with a P row, work 5 rows in st-st. Slip sts on to a spare needle.

Right front: Work as for left front until picot row has been completed. Beginning with a P row, work 4 rows in st-st. *Next row*: P until 5 sts remain, K 5. Now work in pattern with g-st border, as follows. *1st row*: K 5, P to end. *2nd and following 5 alternate rows*: P until 5 sts remain, K 5. *3rd row*: K 6, * YF, sl 1, K 2 tog, PSSO, YF, K 1; repeat from * to end. *5th and 7th rows*: K 6, * YF, sl 1, K 2 tog, PSSO, YF, K 5; repeat from * ending last repeat K 1. *9th row*: K 9, * YF, sl 1, K 1, PSSO, K 1, K 2 tog, YF, K 3; repeat from * until 1 st remains, K 1. *11th row*: as 3rd row. *13th row*: as 1st row.

14th to 20th rows: maintaining g-st border and beginning with a P row, work 7 rows in st-st. Repeat from ** on left front to end.

Sleeves (both alike): Using 3mm needles, cast on 41 sts and work as for back until picot row has been completed. Beginning with a P row, work 4 rows in st-st. *Inc. row*: inc, P 1, inc, P until 3 sts remain, inc, P 1, inc. 45 sts. Change to 3¼mm needles and work 2 patterns as for back, then first 13 rows again. Mark both ends of row. Beginning with a P row, work 5 rows in st-st. Slip sts on to a spare needle.

Yoke: *1st row*: Using long 3mm needles, across sts of right front K 6 then K 2 tog 26 (30) times, across first sleeve K 2 tog 2 (3) times, K 37 (33), K 2 tog 2 (3) times, across back K 1, then K 2 tog 46 (50) times, across second sleeve K 2 tog 2 (3) times, K 35 (31), K 2 tog 3 (4) times, across left front K 2 tog 26 (30) times, K 6. 192 (200) sts. *2nd row*: K. *3rd (buttonhole) row*: K 1, K 2 tog, YF, K to end. *4th and 5th rows*: K. *6th row*: K 5, P until 5 sts remain, K 5. *7th row*: K 19 (18), * sl 1, K 1, PSSO, K 2 tog, K 11 (12); repeat from * until 8 (6) sts remain, K to end. 170 (178) sts. *8th to 12th rows*: maintaining g-st borders, work 5 rows in st-st. *13th (buttonhole) row*: K 1, K 2 tog, YF, K 15 (14), * sl 1, K 1, PSSO, K 2 tog, K 9 (10); repeat from * until 9 (7) sts remain, K to end. 148 (156) sts. *14th to 18th rows*: st-st 5 rows, with g-st borders. *19th row*: K 17 (16), * sl 1, K 1, PSSO, K 2 tog, K 7 (8); repeat from * until 10 (8) sts remain, K to end. 126 (134) sts. *20th, 21st and 22nd rows*: work 3 rows straight. *23rd (buttonhole) row*: K 1, K 2 tog, YF, K 13 (12), * sl 1, K 1, PSSO, K 2 tog, K 5 (6); repeat from * until 11 (9) sts remain, K to end. 104 (112) sts. *24th, 25th and 26th rows*: work 3 rows straight. *27th row*: K 15 (14), * sl 1, K 1, PSSO, K 2 tog, K 3 (4); repeat from * until 12 (10) sts remain, K to end. 82 (90) sts. *28th row*: work straight. *29th row*: K 10

(11), * K 2 tog, K 18 (20); repeat from * ending last repeat K 10 (11). 78 (86) sts. *30th, 31st and 32nd rows*: K 3 rows. *33rd (slot) row*: K 6 (4), * YF, K 2 tog, K 3; repeat from * until 2 sts remain, K 2. K 3 rows. Cast off.

To make up: Press pieces lightly on wrong side, using cool iron over dry cloth. Join side and sleeve seams to markers, then remaining sections of sleeves to remaining sections of armholes. Turn up first 4 rows around lower edge and sleeves and sl-st cast-on edges to wrong side. Press seams. Sew on buttons. Thread narrow ribbon through slot row at neck edge.

BONNET

To work: Using a pair of 3mm needles, cast on 77 (85) sts and work as for back of coat until picot row has been completed. Beginning with a P row, work 5 rows in st-st. Change to a pair of 3¼mm needles and work 20 rows in pattern as on back, then first 14 rows again. Continue in st-st until work measures 10 (11)cm from picot row, ending with a P row and decreasing 1 st at end of last row. 76 (84) sts. **To shape crown:** *1st row*: K 2, * sl 1, K 1, PSSO, K 14 (16), K 2 tog; repeat from * 3 times, K 2. 68 (76) sts. *2nd and following alternate row*: K. *3rd row*: K 2, * sl 1, K 1, PSSO, K 12 (14), K 2 tog; repeat from * 3 times, K 2. *5th row*: K 2, * sl 1, K 1, PSSO, K 10 (12), K 2 tog; repeat from * 3 times, K 2. Continue to dec in this way on every right-side row until 20 (28) sts remain. *Next row*: K 2 tog 10 (14) times. 10 (14) sts. *Following row*: K 2 tog 5 (7) times. Break yarn and thread through remaining sts; draw up closely; fasten off securely on wrong side. *To make up*: Press as for coat. Join back seam from top of crown to beginning of shaping. Turn up first 4 rows along face edge and slip-st cast-on edge to wrong side. Press seams. Using crochet hook, work 1 row of DC along neck edge. Sew wide ribbon to each side.

BOOTEES

To work (both alike): Using 3mm needles, cast on 37 (39) sts and K 1 row. **To shape sole:** *1st row*: K 1, inc, K 15 (16), inc, K 1, inc, K 15 (16), inc, K 1. 41 (43) sts. *2nd and following alternate row*: K. *3rd row*: K. *4th row*: K 2, inc, K 15 (16), inc, K 3, inc, K 15 (16), inc, K 2. *5th row*: K 3, inc, K 15 (16), inc, K 5, inc, K 15 (16), inc, K 3. Continue to inc in this way on every alternate row until there are 61 (63) sts. **Foot:** *1st row (wrong side)*: K. *2nd row*: P. *3rd row*: K. *4th row*: K. *5th row*: P. *6th and 7th rows*: as 4th and 5th rows. *8th and 9th rows*: K. *10th row*: P. *11th to 13th rows*: as 8th to 10th rows. *14th row*: K. **To shape foot:** *1st row (wrong side)*: P 28 (29), P 2 tog, P 1, P 2 tog TBL, P 28 (29). 59 (61) sts. *2nd row*: K 27 (28), sl 1, K 1, PSSO, K 1, K 2 tog, K 27 (28). *3rd row*: P 26 (27), P 2 tog, P 1, P 2 tog TBL, P 26 (27). *4th row*: K 25 (26), sl 1, K 1, PSSO, K 1, K 2 tog, K 25 (26). Continue to dec in this way on every row until 41 (43) sts remain. *Next row (wrong side)*: Inc, P until 1 st remains, inc. 43 (45) sts. *Slot row*: K 1 (2), * YF, K 2 tog, K 1; repeat from * to end (until 1 st remains, K 1). P 1 row, increasing 1 st at both ends of row on 1st size only. 45 sts. Work first 13 pattern rows as on back of coat. Beginning with a P row work 3 rows in st-st. *Picot row*: K 2, * YF, K 2 tog; repeat from * until 1 st remains, K 1. P 1 row, then K 1 row. Cast off.

To make up: Press as for coat. Join leg and underfoot seams. Fold last 2 rows to wrong side; slip-st cast-off edge into place. Press. Thread narrow ribbon through slots.

MITTS

To work (both alike): Using 3mm needles, cast on 45 sts and work as for back of coat until picot row has been completed. Beginning with a P row, work 5 rows in st-st, then work first 13

pattern rows as on back of coat. P 1 row. *Slot row*: K 2, * YF, K 2 tog, K 1; repeat from * until 1 st remains, K 1. *Next row*: P 4, * P 2 tog, P 4 (7); repeat from * until 5 sts remain, P 2 tog, P 3. 38 (40) sts. Continue in st-st until work measures 5 (6)cm from slot row, ending with a P row. **To shape top:** *1st row*: * K 1, sl 1, K 1, PSSO, K 13 (14), K 2 tog, K 1; repeat from * once. *2nd and following 2 alternate rows*: P. *3rd row*: * K 1, sl 1, K 1, PSSO, K 11 (12), K 2 tog, K 1; repeat from * once. *5th row*: * K 1, sl 1, K 1, PSSO, K 9 (10), K 2 tog, K 1; repeat from * once. *7th row*: * K 1, sl 1, K 1, PSSO, K 7 (8), K 2 tog, K 1; repeat from * once, 22 (24) sts. *8th row*: P. Cast off.

To make up: Press as for coat. Join side and top seam. Turn up first 4 rows and slip-st cast-on edge to wrong side. Press seams. Thread narrow ribbon through slots.

SHAWL

To work: Using a pair of 3¼mm needles, cast on 361 sts and K 17 rows. Now work in pattern, with g-st borders, as follows. *1st row (right side)*: K. *2nd row*: K 10, until 10 sts remain, K 10. *3rd to 6th rows*: repeat 1st and 2nd rows twice. *7th and 8th rows*: As 2nd row. *9th row*: K 11, * YF, sl 1, K 2 tog, PSSO, YF, K 1; repeat from * until 10 sts remain, K 10. *10th and following 3 alternate rows*: As 2nd row. *11th and 13th rows*: K 11, * YF, sl 1, K 2 tog, PSSO, YF, K 5; repeat from * until 6 sts remain, K 6. *15th row*: K 14, * YF, sl 1, K 1, PSSO, K 1, K 2 tog, YF, K 3; repeat from * until 11 sts remain, K 11. *17th row*: as 9th row. *18th, 19th and 20th rows*: As 2nd row. These 20 rows form pattern. Repeat them 22 times and first 5 rows again. K 17 rows. Cast off. Press as for coat.

A dress and sweater to keep them warm

Two for toddlers (dress and sweater)

Materials: Patons Trident 4-ply. **Dress (for any one size):** 4 (25g) balls in main colour; 4 balls in 1st contrast; 2 balls in 2nd contrast. **Sweater (for any one size):** 4 (25g) balls in main colour; 4 balls in 1st contrast; 2 balls in 2nd contrast. For best results it is essential to use recommended yarn. Pair each $3\frac{1}{4}$mm and $2\frac{3}{4}$mm needles.

Measurements: To fit 51 (56, 61)cm chest. **Dress:** Length—36 (42, 48)cm, adjustable, sleeve seam — 18 (22, 26)cm, adjustable. **Sweater:** Length—29 (33, 37)cm; sleeve seam—as dress. Figures in brackets refer to larger sizes.

Tension: 17 sts to 5cm in width over slightly stretched rib, using $3\frac{1}{4}$mm needles.

Abbreviations: K—knit; P—purl; st(s)—stitch(es); cm—centimetres; tog—together; inc—increase, by working into front and back of same st; dec—decrease, by working 2 sts tog; TBL—through back of loop(s); single rib is K 1 and P 1 alternately; M—main; A—1st contrast; B—2nd contrast.

DRESS

Back: Using $3\frac{1}{4}$mm needles and M, cast on 134 (146, 158) sts and work in rib as follows. *1st row (wrong side):* P 2, * K 4, P 2; repeat from * to end. *2nd row:* K. Repeat these 2 rows until work measures 12 (14, 17)cm from cast-on edge, ending with a K row. *1st dec row:* P 2, * K 2, K 2 tog, P 2; repeat from * to end. 112 (122, 132) sts. *Next row:* K. *Following row:* P 2, * K 3, P 2; repeat from * to end. Repeat last 2 rows 3 (5, 7) times. K 1 row. *2nd dec row:* P 2, * K 1, K 2 tog, P 2; repeat from * to end. 90 (98, 106) sts. *Next row:* K. *Following row:* P 2, * K 2, P 2; repeat from * to end. Repeat last 2 rows until work measures 17 (22, 27)cm from cast-on edge, ending with a wrong-side row. Fasten off M. Join in A and K 1 row. *Next row:* P 2, * K 2, P 2; repeat from * to end. Rib 13 rows more, as set on last 2 rows. Fasten off A. Join in B and K 1 row, then rib 15 rows. Fasten off B and join

in A. **To shape raglan armholes:** *1st row:* Cast off 4, K to end. *2nd row:* Cast off 4, rib to end. *3rd row:* K 1, K 2 tog TBL, rib until 3 sts remain, K 2 tog, K 1. *4th row:* P 1, P 2 tog, rib until 3 sts remain, P 2 tog TBL, P 1. *5th row:* As 3rd row. *6th row:* P 2, rib until 2 sts remain, P 2. 76 (84, 92) sts. Repeat 3rd to 6th rows 8 (9, 10) times. Slip remaining 28 (30, 32) sts on to a spare needle.

Front: Work as given for back until first 6 rows of armhole shaping have been completed. 76 (84, 92) sts. Repeat 3rd to 6th shaping rows 5 (6, 7) times. 46 (48, 50) sts. *Divide sts for neck: Next row:* K 1, K 2 tog TBL, rib 12, turn and work on these 14 sts, slipping remaining sts on to a spare needle. **Left front shoulder:** Continue to dec 1 st at armhole edge as before, dec 1 st at neck edge on next row and every following alternate row until 5 sts remain. Dec 1 st at armhole edge only on next 3 rows. Work 1 row straight. K 2 tog and fasten off. With right side of work facing, slip next 16 (18, 20) sts on to a spare needle, rejoin yarn to remaining sts, rib until 3 sts remain. K 2 tog, K 1. 14 sts. **Right front shoulder:** Work as given for left front shoulder.

Sleeves (both alike): Using $2\frac{3}{4}$mm needles and B, cast on 38 (44, 50) sts. *1st row:* K 2, * P 1, K 2; repeat from * to end. *2nd row:* P 2, * K 1, P 2; repeat from * to end. Repeat these 2 rows 7 (11, 13) times and 1st row again. *Inc row:* P 2, * inc, P 2; repeat from * to end. 50 (58, 66) sts. Fasten off B. Change to $3\frac{1}{4}$mm needles, join in A and K 1 row. Continue as follows: *1st row (wrong side):* P 2, * K 2, P 2; repeat from * to end. *2nd row:* K 2, * P 2, K 2; repeat from * to end. These 2 rows form rib pattern. Continue in rib, increasing 1 st at both ends of next row and every following 5th row until there are 66 (74, 82) sts. Continue straight until sleeve seam measures 18 (22, 26)cm, or length required, ending with a wrong-side row. Fasten off A and join in

M. **To shape raglan top:** Work first 6 rows of back armhole shaping, then repeat 3rd to 6th rows 7 (8, 9) times and 3rd and 4th rows again. 6 (8, 10) sts. Work 2 rows straight. Leave sts on a safety-pin.

Neckband: Leaving left back raglan open, set in sleeve tops. With right side of work facing, using $2\frac{3}{4}$mm needles and A, K 6 (8, 10) sts from left sleeve top, pick up and K 11 sts from neck edge of left front shoulder, K 16 (18, 20) sts from centre front, pick up and K 11 sts from right front shoulder, K 6 (8, 10) sts from right sleeve, then 28 (30, 32) sts from back. 78 (86, 94) sts. Work 7 rows in single rib. P 1 row on right side to mark hemline, then rib 6 rows more. Cast off neckband very loosely in rib.

To make up: Press pieces lightly on wrong side, using warm iron over damp cloth. Join remaining raglan, continuing seam across neckband. Join side and sleeve seams. Fold neckband in half at marked hemline and slip-st cast-off edge to wrong side. Damp-press seams.

SWEATER

Back: Using $2\frac{3}{4}$mm needles and M, cast on 90 (98, 106) sts and work in K 2, P 2 rib, as follows: *1st row (right side):* K 2, * P 2, K 2; repeat from * to end. *2nd row:* P 2, * K 2, P 2; repeat from * to end. These 2 rows form rib pattern. Repeat them 6 times. Change to $3\frac{1}{4}$mm needles and continue in rib until work measures 10 (13, 16)cm from cast-on edge, ending with a wrong-side row. Fasten off M. Join in A and K 1 row, then rib 15 rows. Fasten off A. Join in B and repeat last 16 rows. Fasten off B. Join in A and shape armholes and work to end, as for back of dress.

Front: Work as for back until armhole shaping is reached. Join in A and shape armholes and work to end, as for front of dress.

Sleeves, neckband and making up: As for dress.

Six-size sweater

Materials 7 (8, 10, 12, 13, 15) 20g balls Lister Concorde Easy Wash Double Knitting. For best results it is essential to use recommended yarn. Pair each 3¾mm and 3mm needles; 1 cable needle.

Measurements: To fit 56 (61, 66, 71, 76, 82)cm chest. Length from shoulder—36 (38, 40, 43, 46, 48)cm; sleeve seam (including cuff) —30 (34, 39, 43, 46, 47)cm. Figures in brackets refer to larger sizes.

Tension: 12 sts to 5cm in width over reversed st-st using 3¾mm needles.

Abbreviations: K—knit; P—purl; st(s)—stitch(es); cm—centimetres; tog—together; inc—increase, by working into front and back of same st; dec—decrease, by working 2 sts tog; sl—slip; PSSO—pass slipped st over; single rib is K 1 and P 1 alternately; C 2F—cable 2 forward: slip next st on to a cable needle and leave at front of work, K 1, then K 1 from cable needle; C 2B—cable 2 back: slip next st on to a cable needle and leave at back of work, K 1, then K 1 from cable needle.

Back: Using 3mm needles, cast on 68 (74, 80, 86, 92, 98) sts and work 18 (18, 18, 22, 22, 22) rows in single rib, inc 1 st at end of last row on 3rd and 4th sizes only. 68 (74, 81, 87, 92, 98) sts. Change to 3¾mm needles and pattern. *1st row (right side) :* P 20 (23, 23, 26, 25, 28), ★ P 1, C 2F, K 1, C 2B, P 1; repeat from ★ 3 (3, 4, 4, 5, 5) times, P to end. *2nd row :* K 20 (23, 23, 26, 25, 28), ★ K 1, P 5, K 1; repeat from ★ 3 (3, 4, 4, 5, 5) times, K to end. *3rd row :* P 20 (23, 23, 26, 25, 28), ★ P 1, C 2B, K 1, C 2F, P 1; repeat from ★ 3 (3, 4, 4, 5, 5) times, P to end. *4th row :* As 2nd row. These 4 rows form the pattern. Continue straight in pattern until work measures 22 (23, 24, 25, 27, 28)cm from cast-on edge ending with a wrong side row. **To shape raglan armholes:** Cast off 2 (2, 3, 3, 3, 3) sts at the beginning of the next 2 rows. *3rd row :* K 2, sl 1, K 1, PSSO, pattern to last 4 sts, K 2 tog, K 2. *4th row :* K 1, P 2, pattern to last 3 sts, P 2,

K 1. Repeat 3rd and 4th rows until 22 (24, 25, 27, 28, 30) sts remain. Leave these sts on a stitch holder.

Front: Work as for back until 42 (44, 45, 47, 52, 54) sts remain in armhole shaping, ending with a wrong side row. **To shape neck:** *next row :* K 2, sl 1, K 1, PSSO, pattern 11 (11, 11, 11, 13, 13) turn.

Left front shoulder: *1st row :* pattern to last 3 sts, P 2, K 1. *2nd row :* K 2, sl 1, K 1, PSSO, pattern to last 3 sts, K 2 tog, K 1. Repeat the last 2 rows until 6 (6, 6, 6, 8, 8) sts remain. Keeping neck edge straight continue to dec at armhole edge as before until 2 sts remain, working dec at outer edge when they can no longer be worked inside a border. Work 2 tog and fasten off. With right side of work facing slip centre 12 (14, 15, 17, 18, 20) sts on to a spare needle, rejoin yarn to remaining sts, pattern to last 4 sts, K 2 tog, K 2. **Right front shoulder:** complete to match left front shoulder reversing all shapings.

Sleeves (both alike): Using 3mm needles cast on 36 (36, 40, 40, 44, 44) sts and work 36 (36, 36, 44, 44, 44) rows in single rib, dec 1 st at end of last row on 3rd and 4th sizes only. 36 (36, 39, 39, 44, 44) sts. Change to 3¾mm needles and pattern. *1st row (right side) :* P 11 (11, 9, 9, 8, 8), ★ P 1, C 2F, K 1, C 2B, P 1; repeat from ★ once (once, 2, 2, 3, 3) times, P to end. *2nd row :* K 11 (11, 9, 9, 8, 8), ★ K 1, P 5, K 1; repeat from ★ once (once, 2, 2, 3, 3) times, K to end. *3rd row :* P 11, (11, 9, 9, 8, 8), ★ P 1, C 2B, K 1, C 2F, P 1; repeat from ★ once (once, 2, 2, 3, 3) times, P to end. *4th row :* as 2nd row. These 4 rows set the pattern. Continue in pattern, inc and work into reversed st-st, 1 st at each end of the next and every following 8th (6th, 8th, 6th, 8th, 6th) row until there are 52 (56, 61, 65, 70, 74) sts. Continue without further shaping until seam measures 30 (34, 39, 43, 46, 47)cm from cast-on edge ending with a wrong side row. **To shape raglan top:** Cast off 2 (2, 3, 3, 3, 3) sts at the beginning of the next 2 rows. *3rd row :* K 2, ★ sl 1, K 1, PSSO,

pattern to last 4 sts, K 2 tog, K 2. *4th row :* K 1, P 2, pattern to last 3 sts, P 2, K 1. Repeat 3rd and 4th rows until 6 (6, 7, 7, 6, 6) sts remain. **3rd and 4th sizes only:** *next row :* K 2, sl 1, K 2 tog, K 2. *Next row :* K 1, P to last st, K 1. **All sizes:** leave remaining 6 (6, 5, 5, 6, 6) sts on a spare needle.

Neckband: Join raglan seams, leaving left back seam open. With right side of work facing, using 3mm needles K across 6 (6, 5, 5, 6, 6) sts on top of left sleeve, pick up and K 20 (20, 20, 20, 24, 24) sts down left side of front neck, K across 12 (14, 15, 17, 18, 20) sts at centre front, pick up and K 20 (20, 20, 20, 24, 24) sts up right front neck, K across 6 (6, 5, 5, 6, 6) sts on top of right sleeve, K across 22 (24, 25, 27, 28, 30) sts on back neck. 86 (90, 90, 94, 106, 110) sts. **Crew neck:** work 8 rows in single rib. **Polo neck:** work 32 rows in single rib. **Both versions:** Cast off loosely in rib.

To make up: Join remaining raglan seam. Join side and sleeve seams.

Detail of stitching

46

Light and lacy (evening top)

Materials: 11 (11, 12) 25g balls Jaeger 3-ply wool. For best results it is essential to use recommended yarn. Pair each 3mm, 2¾mm and 2¼mm knitting needles; 2·50mm crochet hook.

Measurements: To fit 87 (92, 97) cm bust. Length – 55 (56, 57) cm; sleeve seam 43cm. Figures in brackets refer to larger sizes.

Tension: 16sts—2 repeats of pattern, to 5cm in width, using 3mm needles.

Abbreviations: K—knit; P—purl; st(s)—stitch(es); cm—centimetres; tog—together; inc—increase, by working into front and back of same st; dec—decrease, by working 2 sts tog; single rib is K 1 and P 1 alternately; YF—yarn forward, to make 1 st; PSSO—pass slipped st over; CH-chain; DC—double crochet.

Back: Using 2¼mm needles, cast on 143 (151, 159) sts and work in single rib, as follows. *1st row (right side)*: K 2, ★ P 1, K 1; repeat from ★ until 3 sts remain, P 1, K 2. *2nd row*: K 1, ★ P 1, K 1; repeat from ★ to end. Repeat these 2 rows until work measures 5cm from cast-on edge. Change to 2¾mm needles and rib 8cm more. Change to 3mm needles and rib a further 7cm, ending with a wrong-side row and decreasing 1 st at both ends of last row. 141 (149, 157) sts. Continue in lacy pattern, as follows. *1st row (right side)*: K 1, ★ YF, slip 1, K 2 tog, PSSO, YF, K 5; repeat from ★ until 4 sts remain, YF, slip 1, K 2 tog, PSSO, YF, K 1. *2nd and following 2 alternate rows*: P. *3rd row*: as 1st row. *5th row*: K 4, ★ YF, slip 1, K 1, PSSO, K 1, K 2 tog, YF, K 3; repeat from ★ until 1 st remains, K 1. *7th row*: K 1, ★ YF, slip 1, K 2 tog, PSSO, YF, K 1; repeat from ★ until 4 sts remain, YF, slip 1, K 2 tog, PSSO, YF, K 1. *8th row*: P. These 8 rows form pattern. Repeat them until the work measures 35cm from the cast-on edge, ending with a wrong-side row.

To shape armholes: Cast off 8 (8, 9) sts at beginning of next 2 rows. Dec 1 st at both ends of every row until 109 (109, 117) sts remain. Continue straight until work measures 19 (20, 21)cm from beginning of armhole shaping, ending with a wrong-side row. **To slope shoulders**: Cast off 7 (7, 8) sts at beginning of next 8 rows. Cast off remaining 53 sts.

Front: Work as given for back until first 2 rows of lacy pattern have been completed. Divide sts for front opening: *next row*: pattern 25 (33, 33) and slip these sts on to a spare needle, pattern to end and work on these 116 (116, 124) sts. **Right front**: Continuing in pattern, dec 1 st at front edge on next row and every following alternate row, at same time, when work measures same as back to armholes, ending at side-seam edge, shape armhole by casting off 8 (8, 9) sts at beginning of next row. Dec 1 st at armhole edge on next 8 (12, 11) rows. Keeping armhole edge straight, continue to dec at front edge on every alternate row until 28 (28, 32) sts remain. Continue straight until work measures same as back to shoulders, ending at armhole edge. **To slope shoulder**: Cast off 7 (7, 8) sts at beginning of next row and following 3 alternate rows. Fasten off. With wrong side of work facing, rejoin yarn to remaining 25 (33, 33) sts, cast on 90 (82, 90), pattern to end. 115 (115, 123) sts. **Left front**: Work as for right front, reversing all shaping.

Sleeves (both alike): Using 2¼mm needles, cast on 69 (69, 77) sts and work 32 rows in single rib. Change to 2¾mm needles and work 10 rows in lacy pattern, as on back. Continue in pattern and inc 1 st at both ends of next row and every following 6th row until there are 109 (109, 117) sts. Continue straight until sleeve seam measures 43cm, or length required, ending with a wrong-side row. **To shape top**: Cast off 8 (8, 9) sts at beginning of next 2 rows. Dec 1 st at beginning of next 4 rows. Cast off 2 sts at beginning of next 38 rows, then 2 (2, 3) sts on following 4 rows. Cast off remaining 5 (5, 7) sts.

To make up: Press pieces lightly on wrong side, using warm iron over damp cloth. Join shoulder seams. Set in sleeves, then join side and sleeve seams. Sew cast-on sts of left front opening behind right front. With right side of work facing, using crochet hook and beginning at opening, work 1 row of DC evenly up right front, around back of neck and down left front. Fasten off. Place a coloured marker on left front at point where right front crosses over.

Edging: With right side of work facing and using crochet hook, beginning at lower edge of right front opening, slip st into 1st DC, ★ 3 CH, miss 2 DC, 1 DC into next DC; repeat from ★ to marker on left front, turn. *Next row*: ★ into next 3-CH loop work 4 CH/1 DC/ 4 CH/1 DC/4 CH/1 DC; repeat from ★ to end. *Following row*: work 5 CH and 1 DC into each 4-CH loop. Fasten off.

To complete: Secure right front to left front with a few sts from marker to beginning of opening, then catch down row ends of edging on right front, to top of ribbing. Press seams.

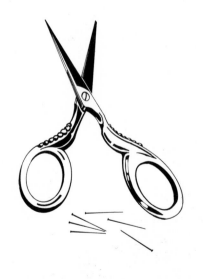

48

Long evening coat

Materials: 13 (14) 50g balls Barbara by 3 Suisses. For best results it is essential to use recommended yarn. Pair each 5½mm, 4½mm and 3¾mm needles. 1·75mm crochet hook.

Measurements: To fit 87–89 (91–94)cm bust; 91–94 (97–99)cm hips. Length—131 (132)cm; sleeve seam—39cm. Figures in brackets refer to larger size.

Tension: 11 sts to 5cm in width over main pattern, using 3¾mm needles.

Abbreviations: K—knit; P—purl; st(s)—stitch(es); tog—together; YF—yarn forward, so that it passes over needle before working next st; YAN—yarn around needle to make a st; TBL—through back of loops; up 1—pick up loop that lies between needles, slip it on to left-hand needle and K into back of it; dec—decrease, by working 2 sts tog; K 1 double—K 1, winding yarn twice around needle; CH—chain; DC—double crochet; SS—slip st; cm—centimetres.

Back: Using 3¾mm needles, cast on 183 (191) sts and K 1 row. Now work in main pattern, as follows. *1st row (right side):* K 1, ★ K 2 tog; repeat from ★ to end. *2nd row:* ★ K 1 double into thread that lies between sts, K 1 double into next st; repeat from ★ to end. *3rd row:* All K, dropping extra loops. 183 (191) sts. *4th, 5th and 6th rows:* P 3 rows. These 6 rows form pattern. Repeat them until work measures about 41cm, ending with a 3rd pattern row. *1st dec row:* P 12 (16), ★ P 2 tog, P 2 tog, P 10; repeat from ★ 10 times, P 2 tog, P 2 tog, P 13 (17). 159 (167) sts. Continue straight in pattern until work measures about 84cm ending with a 3rd pattern row. *3rd dec row:* P 10 (14), ★ P 2 tog, P 2 tog, P 6; repeat from ★ 10 times, P 2 tog, P 2 tog, P 11 (15). 111 (119) sts. Continue straight in pattern until work measures about 97cm when hanging up. *4th dec row:* P 4 (8), ★ P 2 tog, P 2 tog, P 10; repeat from ★ 6 times, P 2 tog, P 2 tog. P 5 (9). 95 (103) sts. P 1 row. Cast off loosely purlwise, but do not fasten off last st. Turn and, on to same needle, pick up and K 94 (102) sts over those cast off. 95 (103) sts. K 1 row, then, beginning with a 1st pattern row, work 7·5cm in pattern, ending with a 6th row of pattern. **To shape armholes:** *1st row:* Cast off 4, ★ K 2 tog; repeat from ★ until 4 sts remain, K 4. *2nd row:* Cast off 4, repeat from ★ of 2nd pattern row to end.

3rd row: All K, dropping extra loops. ** *4th row:* P 2 tog, P to last 2 sts, P 2 tog. *5th row:* P. *6th row:* As 4th row. *7th to 9th rows:* As 1st to 3rd rows of straight pattern. Repeat from **, decreasing, as before, at both ends of 4th and 6th pattern rows, until 75 (79) sts remain. Continue straight until work measures 18 (19) cm from beginning of armhole shaping, ending with a 6th pattern row. **To slope shoulders:** *1st row:* Cast off 6, * K 2 tog; repeat from * until 6 sts remain, K 6. *2nd row:* Cast off 6, repeat from * of 2nd pattern row to end. *3rd row:* Cast off 6, K to end, dropping extra loops. *4th row:* Cast off 6, P to end. Cast off 11 (13) sts at beginning of next 2 rows. Cast off remaining 29 sts loosely.

Left front: Using 3¾mm needles, cast on 93 (97) sts and work as for back until first dec row is reached. *1st dec row:* P 6, * P 2 tog, P 2 tog, P 10; repeat from * 4 times, P 2 tog, P 2 tog, P 13 (17). 81 (85) sts. Continue in pattern as on back to 2nd dec row. *2nd dec row:* P 5, * P 2 tog, P 2 tog, P 8; repeat from * 4 times, P 2 tog, P 2 tog, P 12 (16). 69 (73) sts. Continue in pattern to 3rd dec row. *3rd dec row:* P 4, * P 2 tog, P 2 tog, P 6; repeat from * 4 times, P 2 tog, P 2 tog, P 11 (15). 57 (61) sts. Continue in pattern to 4th dec row. *4th dec row:* P 6, * P 2 tog, P 2 tog, P 10; repeat from * twice, P 2 tog, P 2 tog, P 5 (9). 49 (53) sts. P 1 row. Cast off loosely purlwise, but do not fasten off last st. Turn and on to same needle pick up and K 48 (53) sts over those cast off. 49 (53) sts. K 1 row, then, beginning with a 1st pattern row, work in pattern until work measures same as back to armholes. **To shape armhole:** *1st row:* Cast off 4, * K 2 tog; repeat from * to end. *2nd row:* As 2nd row of straight pattern. *3rd row:* All K, dropping extra loops. *4th row:* P to last 2 sts, P 2 tog. *5th row:* P. *6th row:* As 4th row. Work 3 rows straight. Continue to dec in this way at armhole edge on 4th and 6th pattern rows until 39 (41) sts remain. Continue straight

until work measures 13 (14)cm from beginning of armhole shaping, ending with a 5th pattern row. **To shape neck:** *Next row:* Cast off 16 sts purlwise, P to end. Continue straight in pattern on remaining 23 (25) sts until armhole measures same as back armhole, ending at armhole edge. **To slope shoulder:** Cast off 6 sts at beginning of next row and following alternate row. Work 1 row straight, then cast off remaining 11 (13) sts. **Right front:** Work to match left front, reversing all shaping.

Sleeves (both alike): Using 5½mm needles, cast on 101 (109) sts and P 1 row. *1st row:* K 1, K 2 tog, YF, * K 6, K 2 tog, YF; repeat from * until 2 sts remain, K 2. *2nd row:* P 3, * YAN, P 2 tog, P 3, P 2 tog TBL, YAN, P 1; repeat from * until 2 sts remain, P 2. *3rd row:* K 4, * YF, K 2 tog TBL, K 1, K 2 tog, YF, K 3; repeat from * until 1 st remains, K 1. *4th row:* P 5, * YAN, P 3 tog, YAN, P 5; repeat from * to end. *5th to 8th rows:* Repeat 1st to 4th rows. *9th row:* * K 6, YF, K 2 tog TBL; repeat from * until 5 sts remain, K 5. *10th row:* P 4, * P 2 tog TBL, YAN, P 1, YAN, P 2 tog, P 3; repeat from * until 1 st remains, P 1. *11th row:* K 3, * K 2 tog, YF, K 3, YF, K 2 tog TBL, K 1; repeat from * until 2 sts remain, K 2. *12th row:* P 2, P 2 tog TBL, YAN, * P 5, YAN, P 3 tog, YAN; repeat from * until 9 sts remain, P 5, YAN, P 2 tog, P 2. *13th to 16th rows:* As 9th to 12th rows. These 16 rows form pattern for sleeves. Continue straight in pattern until work measures 14cm. Change to 4½mm needles and continue straight in pattern until work measures 19cm, then change to 3¾mm needles and continue straight until work measures about 24cm, ending with an 8th or 16th pattern row. *Next row:* K 2 (4), * K 2 tog; repeat from * until 3 (5) sts remain, K 3 (5). 53 (59) sts. Cast off loosely purlwise, but do not fasten off last st. Turn and on to same needle pick up and K 52 (58) sts over those cast off. 53 (59) sts. K 1 row, then work 6 rows in

main pattern, as given on back. Repeat 1st to 3rd rows again. *Next row:* P 1, up 1, P until 1 st remains, up 1, P 1, P 2 rows. *Next row:* K 2, * K 2 tog; repeat from * until 1 st remains, K 1. *Next row:* K 1, K 1 double, * K 1 double into thread that lies between sts, K 1 double; repeat from * until 1 st remains, K 1. *Next row:* All K, dropping extra loops. Repeat last 6 rows 5 times. 65 (71) sts. Continue straight in pattern on these sts until work measures 15cm from picked-up edge, ending with a 6th pattern row. **To shape sleeve top:** *1st row:* Cast off 4, * K 2 tog; repeat from * until 4 sts remain, K 4. *2nd row:* Cast off 4, repeat from * of 2nd row of main pattern to end. *3rd row:* All K, dropping extra loops. *4th row:* P 2 tog, P to last 2 sts, P 2 tog. *5th row:* P. *6th row:* As 4th row. Work 3 rows straight in pattern. Continue to dec in this way at both ends of 4th and 6th pattern rows until 33 (39) sts remain, ending with a 6th pattern row. Now continue shaping, as follows: *1st row:* Cast off 2, * K 2 tog; repeat from * until 2 sts remain, K 2. *2nd row:* Cast off 2, repeat from * of 2nd row of main pattern until 2 sts remain, K 2. *3rd row:* Cast off 2, K to end, dropping extra loops. *4th row:* Cast off 2, P to end. Cast off 4 sts at beginning of next 2 rows. Cast off remaining 17 (23) sts.

To make up: Do not press. Join shoulder seams. Set in sleeves, then join side and sleeve seams in one line.

Crochet edging: Beginning at lower edge of right front, work 1 row of DC evenly up right front, around neck edge and down left front, taking care to keep to tension of knitted edge, turn. *Picot row:* SS into 1st DC, * 3 CH, 1 DC into 1st of 3 CH, miss 1 DC, SS into next DC; repeat from * all around. Fasten off. Lightly press seams with a cool iron over dry cloth.

An elegant shawl for day or evening

Stole

Materials: 6 (50g) balls Barbara by 3 Suisses. For best results, it is essential to use recommended yarn. Pair 4½mm needles; 2·50mm crochet hook.

Measurements: Stole will measure about 46cm by 180cm without fringe.
Tension: 2 patterns—16 sts—to 7·5cm in width.

Abbreviations: K—knit; P—purl; st(s)—stitch(es); cm—centimetres; tog—together; sl—slip; YF—yarn forward, so that it passes over needle before working next st, thus making a st; YAN—yarn around needle to make a st; TBL—through back of loops; CH—chain; DC—double crochet.

To work: Using 4½mm needles, cast on 103 sts and P 1 row. Now work in pattern, as follows: *1st row:* Sl 1, K 1, K 2 tog, YF, ★ K 6, K 2 tog, YF; repeat from ★ until 3 sts remain, K 3. *2nd row:* Sl 1, K 1, P 2, ★ YAN, P 2 tog, P 3, P 2 tog, P 2 tog TBL, YAN, P 1; repeat from ★ until 3 sts remain, P 1, K 2. *3rd row:* Sl 1, K 4, ★ YF, K 2 tog TBL, K 1, K 2 tog, YF, K 3; repeat from ★ until 2 sts remain, K 2. *4th row:* Sl 1, K 1, P 4, ★ YAN, P 3 tog, YAN, P 5; repeat from ★ until 9 sts remain, YAN, P 3 tog, YAN, P 4, K 2. *5th to 8th rows:* As 1st to 4th rows. *9th row:* Sl 1, ★ K 6, YF, K 2 tog TBL; repeat from ★ until 6 sts remain, K 6. *10th row:* Sl 1, K 1, P 3, ★ P 2 tog TBL, YAN, P 1, YAN, P 2 tog, P 3; repeat from ★ until 2 sts remain, K 3. *11th row:* Sl 1, K 3, ★ K 2 tog, YF, K 3, K 2 tog TBL, K 1; repeat from ★ until 2 sts remain, K 3. *12th row:* Sl 1, K 1, P 1, P 2 tog TBL, YAN, ★ P 5, YAN, P 3 tog, YAN; repeat from ★ until 10 sts remain, P 5, YAN, P 2 tog, P 1, K 2. *13th to 16th rows:* As 9th to 12th rows. These 16 rows form pattern. Continue straight in pattern until work is about 180cm long, ending with a 16th pattern row, K 1 row; cast off.
Edging: Let first 3 and last 3 sts roll on to wrong side to form a double border. Attach yarn to 4th st of cast-on edge, 1 DC into st, ★ 2 CH, miss next st, 1 DC into next st; repeat from ★ to end. Fasten off. Work edging along cast-off edge in same way. Cut remaining yarn into 33cm lengths and, using 3 lengths together, work a tassel into each 2-CH space.

Two-way winner (poncho and skirt)

Materials: Patons Husky: 10 (50g) balls in Main Colour; 3 balls each of 1st and 2nd Contrast Colours. For best results it is essential to use recommended yarn. Pair each of long 6½mm, 6mm and 4½mm needles; 23cm zip.

Measurements: Side seam — 63cm.

Tension: 15 sts to 10cm in width over st-st using 6mm needles.

Abbreviations: K—knit; P—purl; st(s)—stitch(es); cm—centimetres; tog—together; st-st—stocking-stitch, K on right side and P back; YF—yarn forward to make a st; dec—decrease, by working 2 sts tog; TBL—through back of loops; M—Main Colour; A—1st Contrast Colour; B—2nd Contrast Colour. Figures in brackets to be worked number of times stated.

Back and front alike: Using 4½mm needles and A, cast on 186 sts. *1st row (wrong side)*: Using A, K to end. *2nd row*: Using A, K 91, K 2 tog TBL, K 2 tog, K 91. 184 sts. *3rd row*: Using A, K to end. Change to 6 mm needles. *4th row*: Using A, K 90, K 2 tog TBL, K 2 tog, K 90. 182 sts. *5th row*: Using A, P to end. Join in M. *6th row*: Using M, K 89, K 2 tog TBL, K 2 tog, K 89. 180 sts. *7th row*: Using M, P to end. *8th row*: Using M, K 88, K 2 tog TBL, K 2 tog, K 88. 178 sts. *9th row*: Using M, P to end. *10th row*: Using A, K 87, K 2 tog TBL, K 2 tog, K 87. 176 sts. *11th row*: Using A, P to end. *12th row*: K (3A, 1B, 2A) 14 times, 2A, K 2 tog TBL using A, K 2 tog using A, (4A, 1B, 1A) 14 times, 2A. 174 sts. *13th row*: P 2A (3B, 3A), 14 times, 2B, (3A, 3B) 14 times, 2A. *14th row*: K (1A, 5B) 14 times, 1A, K 2 tog TBL using B, K 2 tog using B, 1A (5B, 1A) 14 times. 172 sts. Break off A. Change to 6mm needles. *15th row*: Using B, P to end. *16th row*: Using M, K 84, K 2 tog TBL, K 2 tog, K 84. 170 sts. *17th row*: Using

M, P to end. Change to 6½mm needles. *18th row*: K (4M, 2B) 13 times, 4M, 1B, K 2 tog TBL using B, K 2 tog using M, 2M, (2B, 4M) 13 times, 2B, 1M. 168 sts. *19th row*: P 1M, 2B, (4M, 2B) 13 times, 3M, 2B, 4M, (2B, 4M) 13 times. *20th row*: K (4M, 2B) 13 times, 4M, K 2 tog TBL using B, K 2 tog using M, 1M, (2B, 4M) 13 times, 2B, 1M. 166 sts. *21st row*: P 1M, 2B, (4M, 2B) 13 times, 2M, 1B, 4M, (2B, 4M) 13 times. *22nd row*: K (4M, 8B) 6 times, 4M, 5B, K 2 tog TBL using B, K 2 tog using M, (8B, 4M) 6 times, 8B, 1M. 164 sts. *23rd row*: P 1M, 8B, (4M, 8B) 6 times, 1M, 6B, 4M, (8B, 4M) 6 times. *24th row*: (4M, 8B) 6 times, 4M, 4B, K 2 tog TBL using B, K 2 tog using B, 7B, (4M, 8B) 6 times, 1M. 162 sts. *25th row*: P 7M, (2B, 10M) 6 times, 2B, 3M, (2B, 10M) 6 times, 2B, 4M. *26th row*: K 4M, (2B, 10M) 6 times, 2B, 1M, K 2 tog TBL using M, K 2 tog using B, (10M, 2B) 6 times, 7M. 160 sts. *27th row*: P 7M, (2B, 10M) 6 times, 1B, 2M, 2B, (10M, 2B) 6 times, 4M. *28th row*: K 1M, (5B, 7M) 6 times, 5B, K 2 tog TBL using M, K 2 tog using M, 6M, (5B, 7M) 6 times. 158 sts. *29th row*: P 7M, (4B, 8M) 6 times, 1M, (4B, 8M) 6 times, 4B, 2M. *30th row*: K 3M, (3B, 9M) 6 times, 2B, K 2 tog TBL using B, K 2 tog using M, 7M, (3B, 9M) 5 times, 3B, 7M. 156 sts. *31st row*: P (7M, 2B, 3M) 6 times, 6M, (2B, 10M) 6 times, 2B, 4M. Change to 6mm needles. *32nd row*: Using M K 76, K 2 tog TBL, K 2 tog, K 76. 154 sts. *33rd row*: Using M P to end. Break off M. *34th row*: Using B K 75, K 2 tog TBL, K 2 tog, K 75. 152 sts. *35th row*: Using B P to end. Change to 6½mm needles. Join in A. *36th row*: K (1B, 3A) 18 times, 1B, 1A, K 2 tog TBL using A, K 2 tog using A, 1A, 1B, (3A, 1B) 18 times. 150 sts. *37th row*: P (1B, 3A) 18 times, 1B, 4A, 1B, (3A, 1B) 18 times. Break off A. *38th row*: Using B K 73, K 2 tog TBL, K 2 tog, K 73. 148 sts. Join in M. *39th row*: P 2M, (1B, 3M) 18 times, (3M, 1B) 18 times, 2M.

40th row: K 2M, (1B, 3M) 17 times, 1B, 1M, K 2 tog TBL using M, K 2 tog using M, 1M, 1B, (3M, 1B) 17 times, 2M. 146 sts. Change to 6mm needles. *41st row*: Using B P to end. *42nd row*: Using B K 71, K 2 tog TBL, K 2 tog, K 71. 144 sts. Join in A. *43rd row*: Using A P to end. *44th row*: Using A, K 70, K 2 tog TBL, K 2 tog, K 70. 142 sts. Break off A. *45th row*: Using B P to end. *46th row*: Using B K 69, K 2 tog TBL, K 2 tog, K 69. 140 sts. Break off B. Continue in st-st and M only, decreasing on every alternate row as before until 102 sts remain, ending with a P row. Join in A and B. Continuing in st-st and decreasing as before work in stripes as follows: 2 rows A, 2 rows B, 2 rows M, 2 rows B, and 2 rows A. 92 sts. Break off A and B. Continue in M as follows. *Next row*: K 44, K 2 tog TBL, K 2 tog, K 44. 90 sts. *Next row*: P to end. *Next row*: K 42, K 3 tog TBL, K 3 tog, K 42 sts. 86 sts. *Next row*: P to end. *Next row*: K 40, K 3 tog TBL, K 3 tog, K 40. 82 sts. *Next row*: P to end. *Next row*: K 38, K 3 tog TBL, K 3 tog, K 38. 78 sts. *Next row*: P to end. Continue to dec 4 sts on every alternate row until 54 sts remain ending with a P row. *Eyelet row*: (K 2, YF, K 2 tog TBL) 6 times, K 3 tog TBL, K 3 tog, (K 2 tog, YF, K 2) 6 times. 50 sts. *Next row*: P to end. Change to 4½mm needles. *Next row*: K 22, K 3 tog TBL, K 3 tog, K 22. 46 sts. *Next row*: K to end. *Next row*: K 20, K 3 tog TBL, K 3 tog, K 20. 42 sts. *Next row*: K to end. *Next row*: K 18, K 3 tog TBL, K 3 tog, K 18. 38 sts. Cast off.

To make up: Press all parts lightly on wrong side following instructions on ball bands. Using 30cm lengths of yarn, join side seams leaving 23cm open at top of left side. Insert zip. Using M and A make a twisted cord 100cm long, put a tassel on each end and thread through holes at neck. Cut remaining M and A into 25cm lengths. Knot 1 strand of each colour into every alternate st along cast-on edge to form a fringe.

This versatile poncho may also be worn as a skirt

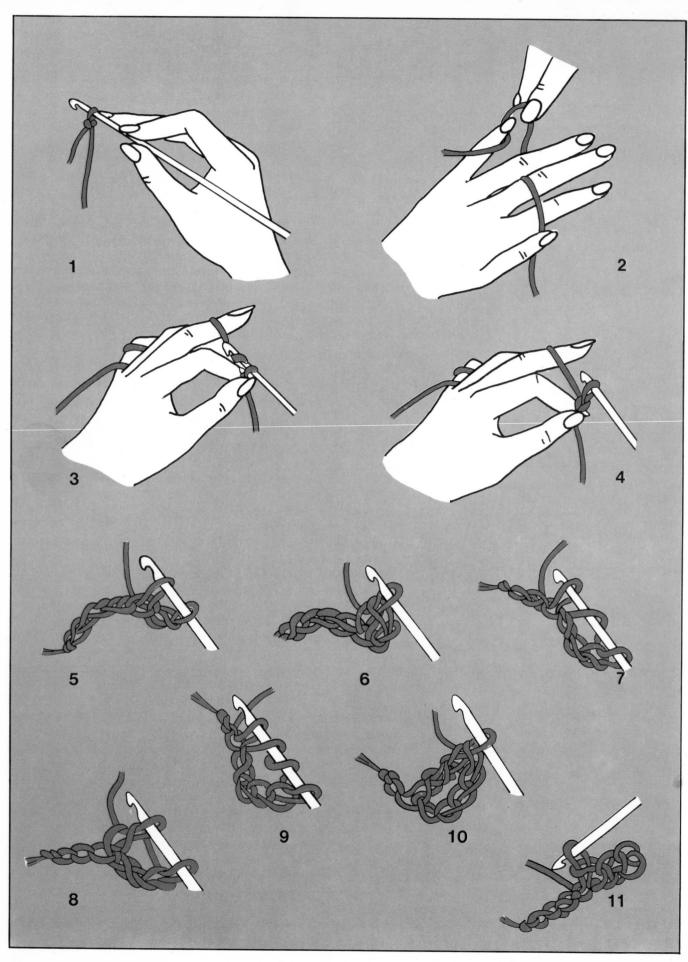

Crochet

How to crochet

Practise these basic crochet stitches, following our step-by-step diagrams.

Chain: This forms the basis of all crochet stitches. Make a slip loop and place it on hook (sketch 1). Wind the yarn over the forefinger and middle finger of the left hand, under third finger and around the little finger (sketch 2). * Hold hook between thumb and forefinger of right hand, then, holding base of loop between thumb and forefinger of left hand, take hook under extended yarn, catching up yarn with hook (sketch 3). Draw yarn and head of hook through loop, thus leaving the previous loop below the loop just made (sketch 4). Repeat from * for the required length.

Double crochet: Draw a loop through next stitch (or chain) as in sketch 5, then draw a second loop through both loops now on hook (sketch 6). Repeat for number of stitches required.

Treble: Take hook under, then over yarn, draw a loop through next stitch (sketch 7)—3 loops on hook, draw a loop through first 2 loops on hook (sketch 8)—2 loops now on hook, then draw a loop through remaining 2 loops; repeat for number of stitches required.

Double treble: Take hook under, then over yarn twice, then draw a loop through next stitch (sketch 9) —4 loops on hook. Now work off loops in pairs, as for treble (sketch 10). Repeat for number of stitches required.

Slip-stitch: Insert hook into next stitch, then draw a loop through this stitch and also through the original stitch on hook. (Sketch 11 shows the finished stitch.) Repeat for number of stitches required.

Step-by-step crochet

Note: When turning to start a new row, extra chains are worked to form an upright stitch, to keep a straight edge. The number of chain stitches required depends on the stitch being used, but it is normally included in the crochet pattern. A guide for use when practising is: double crochet—1 turning chain; treble—3 turning chains; double treble—4 turning chains.

Silky party shawl

Materials: 20 (20g) balls Twilley's Lystwist. For best results it is essential to use recommended yarn. 2·00mm crochet hook.

Measurements: Width at base edge 160cm; depth at centre (excluding fringe) approximately 90cm.

Tension: 1 pattern to 10·5cm in width.

Abbreviations: CH—chain; TR —treble; SS—slip-stitch; cm—centimetres. Instructions in brackets should be worked the number of times stated. Yarn must be joined at the beginning of a row. Leave yarn remaining on spools for fringe. Leave 6cm ends and darn in securely. Because of the slippery nature of this yarn it is advisable to wrap the yarn twice around the little finger to obtain an even tension.

To make: Make 422 CH. **Foundation row**: 1 TR in 6th CH from hook, (1 CH, miss 1 CH, 1 TR in next CH) 11 times, * 1 CH, miss 1 CH, 1 TR in each of next 3 CH, (1 CH, miss 1 CH, 1 TR in next CH) 12 times; repeat from * to last 2 CH, 1 CH, miss 1 CH, 1 TR in last CH. Continue in pattern thus: *1st row*: Miss first TR, SS in 1 CH, SS in next TR, 4 CH, 1 TR in next TR, (1 CH, 1 TR in next TR) 10 times, * 1 TR in next CH, 1 TR in each of next 3 TR, 1 TR in next CH, 1 TR in next TR, (1 CH, 1 TR in next TR) 11 times; repeat from * to end. *2nd row*: Miss first TR, SS in 1 CH, SS in next TR, 4 CH, 1 TR in next TR, (1 CH, 1 TR in next TR) 8 times, * 1 TR in next CH, 1 TR in each of next 7 TR, 1 TR in next CH, 1 TR in next TR, (1 CH, 1 TR in next TR) 9 times; repeat from * to end. *3rd row*: Miss first TR, SS in 1 CH, SS in next TR, 4 CH, 1 TR in next TR, (1 CH, 1 TR in next TR) 6 times, * 1 TR in next CH, 1 TR in each of next 11 TR, 1 TR in next CH, 1 TR in next TR, (1 CH, 1 TR in next TR) 7 times; repeat from * to end. *4th row*: Miss first TR, SS in 1 CH, SS in next TR, 4 CH, 1 TR in next TR, (1 CH, 1 TR in next TR) 4 times, * 1 TR in next CH, 1 TR in each of next 15 TR, 1 TR in next CH, 1 TR in next TR, (1 CH, 1 TR in next TR) 5 times; repeat from * to end. *5th row*: Miss first TR, SS in 1 CH, SS in next TR, 4 CH, 1 TR in next TR, (1 CH, 1 TR in next TR) twice, * 1 TR in next CH, 1 TR in each of next 19 TR, 1 TR in next CH, 1 TR in next TR, (1 CH, 1 TR in next TR) 3 times; repeat from * to end. *6th row*: Miss first TR, SS in 1 CH, SS in next TR, 4 CH, 1 TR in next TR, * 1 TR in next CH, 1 TR in each of next 23 TR, 1 TR in next CH, 1 TR in next TR, 1 CH, 1 TR in next TR; repeat from * to end. *7th row*: Miss first TR, SS in 1 CH, SS in next TR, 4 CH, miss next TR, 1 TR in next TR, (1 CH, miss next TR, 1 TR in next TR) 12 times, * 1 TR in next CH, 1 TR in next TR, (1 CH, miss next TR, 1 TR in next TR) 13 times; repeat from * to end. Repeat 1st to 7th pattern rows until 31 sts remain. Shaping work at each end of every row as before, complete by working 1 open-work triangle. Fasten off.

Fringe: * Wrap yarn 6 times around a 13cm strip of strong card and cut end of yarn. Gripping the 6 strands tightly together, carefully remove from card and knot opposite end to cut ends through CH space of row end. Cut ends of strands to form fringe and double knot over top of first knot to secure; repeat from * into each row of both shaped edges.

Detail of stitching

Baby's cape

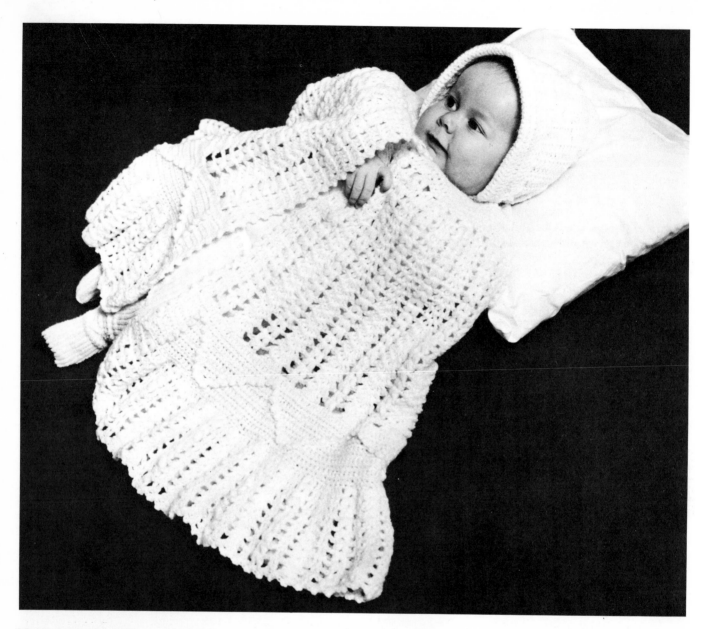

Materials: 13 (20g) balls Sirdar Snuggly Baby Wash and Wear 4-ply. For best results it is essential to use recommended yarn. 3·00mm and 3·50mm crochet hooks; 3 small buttons.

Measurements: Neck edge to hem—56cm; width at lower edge—about 193cm; around face edge of hood—35.5cm.

Tension: 10 TR to 5cm in width, using 3·00mm hook.

Abbreviations: CH — chain; st(s) — stitch(es); cm — centimetres; lp(s) — loop(s); sp(s) — space(s); TR — treble; DC — double crochet; cl(s) — cluster(s);

YAH—yarn around hook. Directions in brackets should be worked number of times stated.

To make: Begin at neck edge. Using 3·00mm hook, make 79 CH loosely. *1st row:* 1 TR into 3rd CH from hook, 1 TR into each CH to end, turn. 78 sts. *2nd row:* 3 CH to stand for first TR, 1 TR into each of next 13 TR, 2 TR into next TR, * 1 TR into each of next 6 TR, 2 TR into next TR; repeat from * until 14 sts remain, 1 TR into each of last 14 TR, turn. *3rd row:* 3 CH, 1 TR into each of next 13 TR, 2 TR into next TR, * 1 TR into each of next 7 TR,

2 TR into next TR; repeat from * until 15 TR remain, 1 TR into each of last 15 TR, turn. *4th row:* 3 CH, 1 TR into each of next 14 TR, 2 TR into next TR, * 1 TR into each of next 8 TR, 2 TR into next TR; repeat from * until 15 TR remain, 1 TR into each of last 15 TR, turn. *5th row:* 3 CH, 1 TR into each of next 14 TR, 2 TR into next TR, * 1 TR into each of next 9 TR, 2 TR into next TR; repeat from * until 16 TR remain, 1 TR into each of last 16 TR, turn. *6th row:* 3 CH, 1 TR into each of next 15 TR, 2 TR into next TR, * 1 TR into each of next 10 TR,

2 TR into next TR; repeat from * until 16 TR remain, 1 TR into each of last 16 TR, turn. *7th row:* 3 CH, 1 TR into each of next 15 TR, 2 TR into next TR, * 1 TR into each of next 11 TR, 2 TR into next TR; repeat from * until 17 TR remain, 1 TR into each of last 17 TR, turn. *8th row:* 3 CH, 1 TR into each of next 6 TR, 2 TR into next TR, * 1 TR into each of next 10 TR, 2 TR into next TR; repeat from * until 8 TR remain, 1 TR into each of last 8 TR, turn. 137 sts. Change to 3.50mm hook. Work in pattern, as follows: *1st row (right side):* 3 CH, 1 TR into each of first 4 TR, * (YAH, insert hook into next TR and draw up a 1cm lp) 3 times into same TR, YAH and draw through all lps—1 cl worked, 1 CH, 1 cl into same TR as last cl, 1 CH, miss 2 TR, 1 TR/1 CH/1 TR into next TR, 1 CH, miss 2 TR; repeat from * until 6 TR remain, 1 cl/1 CH/1 cl into next TR, 1 TR into each of last 5 TR, turn. *2nd row:* 3 CH, 1 TR into each of first 4 TR, * 1 cl/1 CH/1 cl into 1-CH sp between cls on previous row, 1 CH, 1 TR into next CH-sp, 1 TR/1 CH/1 TR into next 1-CH sp—V-st TR worked, 1 TR into next 1-CH sp, 1 CH; repeat from *, ending 1 cl/1 CH/1 cl into 1-CH sp between last cls, 1 TR into each of last 5 TR, turn. *3rd row:* 3 CH, 1 TR into each of first 4 TR, * 1 cl/1 CH/1 cl into 1-CH sp between cls, 1 CH, 1 TR into sp between single TR and V-st TR, 1 TR/1 CH/1 TR into 1-CH sp of V-st TR, 1 TR into sp between V-st TR and single TR, 1 CH; repeat from *, ending 1 cl/1 CH/1 cl into 1-CH space between last cls, 1 TR into each of last 5 TR, turn. *4th to 12th rows:* As 3rd row. *13th row:* 3 CH, 1 TR into each of next 4 TR, * 1 cl/1 CH/1 cl into 1-CH sp between cls, 1 CH, 1 TR into sp between single TR and V-st TR, 2 TR/1 CH/2 TR into 1-CH sp of V-st TR, 1 TR into sp between V-st TR and single TR, 1 CH; repeat from *, ending 1 cl/1 CH/1 cl into 1-CH sp between last cls,

1 TR into each of last 5 TR, turn. *14th to 24th rows:* As 13th row. *Work TR and DC inset. 1st row:* 3 CH, 1 TR into each of next 4 TR, * 1 TR into each of next cl/1 CH/cl, 2 TR into 1-CH sp, 1 TR into each of next 6 TR, 2 TR into 1-CH sp; repeat from *, ending 1 TR into each of next cl/1 CH/cl, 1 TR into each of last 5 TR, turn. *2nd row:* 1 CH to stand for 1st DC, 1 DC into front lp only of each TR to end, turn. *3rd row:* 3 CH to stand for 1st TR, 1 TR into back lp only of each DC to end, turn. Repeat 2nd and 3rd rows 4 times and 2nd row again. Inset completed, continue in pattern. *1st row:* Work into front lp only along row, 3 CH, 1 TR into each of next 5 DC, * 1 cl/1 CH/1 cl into next DC, 1 CH, miss 1 DC, 1 TR into each of next 2 DC, 2 TR/1 CH/2 TR into next DC, 1 TR into each of next 2 TR, 1 CH, miss 1 DC; repeat from * until 6 DC remain, 1 cl/1 CH/1 cl into next DC, 1 TR into each of next 5 DC, turn. *2nd row:* 3 CH, 1 TR into each of next 4 TR, * 1 cl/1 CH/1 cl into 1-CH sp between cls, 1 CH, 1 TR into each of next 2 TR, 2 TR/1 CH/2 TR into 1-CH sp of V-st TR, miss 2 TR of V-st TR, 1 TR into each of next 2 TR, 1 CH; repeat from *, ending 1 cl/1 CH/1 cl into 1-CH sp of last cl, 1 TR into each of last 5 TR, turn. Repeat 2nd row 8 times. Fasten off. *Cord slot row:* With right side facing, using 3·00mm hook, rejoin yarn to foundation CH at neck edge, 4 CH to stand for 1st TR and 1-CH sp, * miss 1 foundation CH, 1 TR into next CH, 1 CH; repeat from *, ending 1 TR into end foundation CH. Fasten off.

Hood—Back: With right side facing, using 3·00mm hook, rejoin yarn to 16th TR on cord slot row. *1st row:* 3 CH to stand for 1st TR, * (2 TR into 1-CH sp, 1 TR into TR) 8 times, turn. 25 sts. *2nd row:* 3 CH, 1 TR into each TR to end, turn. Repeat 2nd row 12 times. Fasten off. **Side:** With right side facing, using 3·00mm hook, miss 6 1-CH sps, rejoin yarn to next TR. *1st row:* 3 CH, 2 TR into

1-CH sp, (1 TR into TR, 2 TR into 1-CH sp) 8 times. 27 sts. *2nd row:* 3 CH, 1 TR into each TR to end, turn. Repeat 2nd row 38 times. Fasten off. Leaving 6 sps free at left side of neck edge, neatly sew CH edge of last row to cord slot row. **Edging:** With right side facing, using 3·00mm hook, rejoin yarn to 1st row end on hood. *1st row:* 1 DC into same place as join, then work 72 TR evenly around row ends at face edge, 1 DC into last st, 1 CH, turn. *2nd row:* 1 DC into first TR, 1 TR into each TR until 1 TR remains, 1 DC into last TR, 1 CH, turn. Repeat 2nd row 3 times. Fasten off. With right side facing, rejoin yarn to first row end on edging. *Picot row:* 3 CH, slip-st to first of 3 CH to form picot, * miss 1 st, 1 DC into next st, picot, miss 2 sts; repeat from *, working last picot into end st. Fasten off.

Front and lower edging: With right side facing, rejoin yarn to 1st free CH from hood on left front. *Picot row:* 1 DC into each CH along top of cord slot row, picot as before at corner of neck edge, * 1 DC into row end, picot *; repeat from * to * down left front, then work along lower edge as on hood, work from * to * up right front, and finally work 1 DC into each CH along top of cord slot row. Fasten off.

Inset picot trimming: With right side facing, using 3.50mm hook, join yarn to the 8th TR on first row of inset. *Picot row:* * Picot as before, 1 DC into next row end; repeat from * along 8th st from edge on inset, then continue working picots on inset forming a zigzag pattern and ending with 1 straight line on the 8th st from other end. Fasten off.

Cord: Using 3·00mm hook and yarn double, make a CH cord 100cm long. Thread cord through slot row, then work 7 TR into each end of cord.

To make up: Do not press. Join back of hood to row ends at side. Turn hood edging over to right side and slip-st into position. Sew on buttons.

Crochet waistcoat and bag

Materials: 1, 50g ball of double knitting in each of 5 shades—A, B, C, D and E—will make both the waistcoat and the bag; 5·00mm crochet hook for waistcoat; 4·00mm crochet hook for bag.
Measurements: Waistcoat to fit 82–87cm bust; length—45cm.
Tension: 7 TR to 5cm; 2 rows to 3cm using 5·00mm crochet hook.

Abbreviations: CH—chain; TR —treble; DC—double crochet; SS—slip-stitch; st(s)—stitch(es); tog—together; cm—centimetres.

WAISTCOAT

To work: Worked from side to side in one piece beginning with right front. Work 1 row in each colour. Fasten off at the end of each row, turn work and join next colour to first TR. With 5·00mm hook and A make 51 CH. *Foundation row:* 1 TR in 4th CH from hook, 1 TR in each CH to end. 49 sts. *1st row (wrong side):* 3 CH, miss first TR; * miss next TR, 1 TR in next TR, 1 TR in missed TR— crossed TR worked; repeat from * to end working last crossed TR in top of 3 CH and last TR. *2nd row:* 3 CH, miss first TR, 1 TR in each TR, 1 TR in top of 3 CH. These 2 rows form pattern. Pattern 3 rows. Neck shaping: *Next row:* make 16 CH, 1 TR in 4th CH from hook, 1 TR in each of next 12 CH, 1 TR in each TR, 1 TR in top of 3 CH. 63 sts. Pattern 6 rows. Armhole shaping: *Next row:* pattern to last 30 sts, turn. 33 sts. Pattern 4 rows. *Next row:* make 32 CH, 1 TR in 4th CH from hook, 1 TR in each of next 28 CH, 1 TR in each TR, 1 TR in top of 3 CH. 63 sts. Pattern 23 rows. Armhole shaping: *Next row:* miss 30 TR, join yarn to next TR, 3 CH, 1 TR in 31 TR, 1 TR in top of 3 CH. Pattern 4 rows. *Next row:* pattern to end, join a short length of same colour to armhole

end of last row, make 30 CH and fasten off. Then with original yarn * miss 1 CH, 1 TR in next CH, 1 TR in missed CH; repeat from * 14 times. 63 sts. Pattern 6 rows. Neck shaping: *Next row:* miss 14 TR and join yarn to next TR, pattern to end. 49 sts. Pattern 5 rows. Fasten off.

To make up: Press work lightly, then join shoulder seams.
Ties (make two): Join B to neck corner of front and make a 36cm length of CH, 1 DC in 2nd CH from hook, 1 DC in each CH to end. Fasten off.

BAG

Back and front alike: With 4·00mm hook and A, make 4 CH. *Foundation round:* 11 TR in 4th CH from hook, SS in top of 3 CH. *1st round:* 3 CH, 3 TR in next TR, * 1 TR in next TR, 3 TR in next TR; repeat from * 4 times, SS to top of 3 CH. Fasten off. *2nd round:* join C to same place as SS, 3 CH, * 1 TR in next TR, 3 TR in next TR, 1 TR in each of next 2 TR; repeat from * 5 times omitting 1 TR at end of last repeat, SS to top of 3 CH. *3rd round:* 3 CH, * 1 TR in each of next 2 TR, 3 TR in next

TR, 1 TR in each of next 3 TR; repeat from * 5 times omitting 1 TR at end of last repeat, SS to top of 3 CH. *4th round:* join E to same place as SS, 3 CH, * 1 TR in each of next 3 TR, 3 TR in next TR, 1 TR in each of next 4 TR; repeat from * 5 times omitting 1 TR at end of last repeat, SS to top of 3 CH. *5th round:* 3 CH, * 1 TR in each of next 4 TR, 3 TR in next TR, 1 TR in each of next 5 TR; repeat from * 5 times omitting 1 TR at end of last repeat, SS to top of 3 CH. Fasten off. *Edging:* with wrong sides tog and working through both loops of back and front, join A to centre TR of any 3 TR group, 1 DC in each TR along 5 sides to centre TR of last 3 TR group, then leaving 6th side open work 1 DC into each TR of front only of 6th side, turn and work 1 DC into each TR of 6th side of back. **Strap:** With A make an 84cm length of CH, 1 DC in 2nd CH from hook, 1 DC in each CH to end. Fasten off. Sew strap to bag at each side of opening. Using 7 strands tog, knot 2 small tassels each in B and C into the 4 corners. Press work lightly, avoiding tassels.

Detail of bag